MY FIRST REFERENCE LIBRARY

WEATHER

by Julie Brown and Robert Brown
Adapted from Theodore Rowland-Entwistle's
Weather and Climate

❧ BELITHA PRESS

First published in Great Britain in 1991 by
Belitha Press Limited
31 Newington Green, London N16 9PU
Copyright © Belitha Press Limited and
Gareth Stevens, Inc. 1991
Illustrations/photographs copyright © in this
format by Belitha Press Limited and Gareth
Stevens, Inc. 1991
ISNB 1 85561 064 7
Typeset by Chambers Wallace, London
Printed in Hong Kong for Imago Publishing

British Library Cataloguing in Publication Data
CIP data for this book is available from the British
Library

Acknowledgements

Photographic credits:

Heather Angel 38 right
Aquila 41 right
British Antarctic Survey 57 right
Biofoto 4
Canadian National 15
John Cleare/Mountain Camera 29 left, 32 left and
    right
Crown copyright 17 top
Department of Electrical Engineering/University of
    Dundee 12
Patrick Eagar 8
ET Archive 37
Sally and Richard Greenhill 5 bottom left
Susan Griggs/Comstock 30, 31
Robert Harding Picture Library 38 left, 41 top, 42
    left, 45, 47 bottom right, 52
Eric and David Hosking 41 bottom left
Hutchinson Library 25, 39 left, 51 top, 53
Frank Lane Picture Agency 14/15
G. V. Mackie 17 bottom
Magnum 39 right, 42/43, 51 bottom, 54, 58/59
S & O Mathews 5 top and centre right
NASA 57 left
Oxford Scientific Films 16, 43 right
Panos Pictures 59 right
Photo Library of Australia 36
Science Photo Library 21, 28, 29 right, 33, 34, 35
Charles Tait 47 top
ZEFA 23

Illustrated by: Oxford Illustrators Ltd (Jonathan
    Soffe, Simon Lindo and Ray Webb) and Eugene
    Fleury

Series editors: Neil Champion and Mark Sachner
Editors: Rachel Cooke and Rita Reitci
Educational consultant: Carolyn Kain
Art director: Frances McKay
Designed by: Groom and Pickerill
Picture research: Ann Usborne
Specialist consultant: Dick File

Contents

Words found in **bold** are explained
in the glossary on pages 60 and 61

What's the Difference?

Arctic Circle

Tropic of Cancer

The Equator

Tropic of Capricorn

Antarctic Circle

Those circles

The map above is marked with imaginary lines that circle the Earth. Along the Equator, day and night are always the same length. Along the Tropic of Cancer, the Sun appears directly overhead on 21 June each year. Along the Tropic of Capricorn, the Sun appears directly overhead on 21 December.

Inside the Arctic and Antarctic circles, there are days when the Sun never sets and others when it never rises. ▲

CHAPTER ONE

WEATHER OR CLIMATE?

Weather and climate are two ways of looking at changes in **temperature**, wind, rain and sunshine. The word weather means day-to-day changes in a certain area. Scientists who study the weather are called **meteorologists**.

The word climate means the usual weather of an area. Scientists who study climate are called **climatologists**. They believe it takes between 30 and

100 years to understand the climate of a place.

Climate changes from area to area. We expect hot, sunny days in the summer in southern France but in northern England the same summer may be hot or cold, dry or wet. So we say these areas have different climates.

Changing climates

Climates all over the world change with time. Only 20,000 years ago, ice covered large areas of Europe, Asia and North America. In the United Kingdom, the ice sheet reached as far south as London. Today, our climate is much warmer than it was. But it is still changing.

▲ These two photographs show how the weather changes from day to day. The top one was taken one April afternoon. The lower one was taken the next morning. It had snowed in the night.

◄ These two beaches were photographed at the same time of year but in places with different climates. Far left: the beach is near the Arctic Circle. The nearer beach is close to the Equator.

What Makes the Weather?

▶ Water moves around the world in what is known as the water cycle. Water vapour rises up from the sea (1) and forms clouds (2). Some of these clouds produce rain (3). If the rain falls on land, the water slowly returns to the sea, for example, in rivers (4).

Air pressure

The weight of air around the Earth presses down on its surface. This is called **air pressure**.

When air becomes warm it also becomes lighter and the pressure changes. This means that air pressure is affected by the Sun's heat. As a result, changing air pressure affects the weather.

CHAPTER TWO

HOW WEATHER WORKS

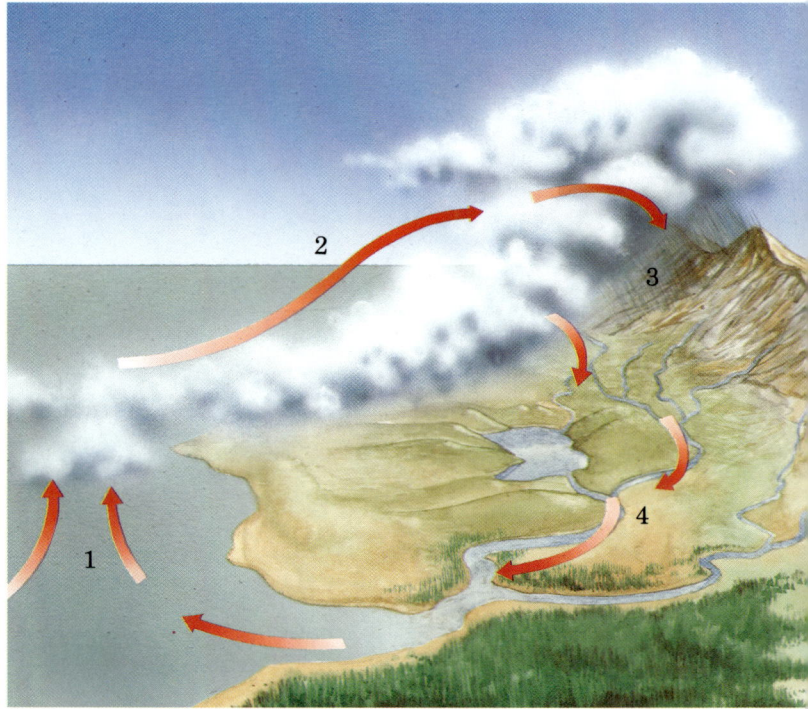

The weather is made by the Sun heating the air which surrounds the Earth. The Sun heats the air differently from area to area. This is because the Earth is round. As a result, the Sun's heat is spread over a small area at the Equator, making it very hot. The same amount of heat is spread over a larger area at the **poles**, so they are much colder.

In the **tropics**, land and sea are always warm. But further north or south, the land is hotter than the sea in summer and colder than the sea in winter.

This affects the temperature of the air. Some areas of air are warm and some are cold. A warm area of air rises away from the Earth and cooler air blows in to take its place. This is the basic cause of winds.

Moving air also causes clouds and rain. Rising air takes water **vapour** from the sea with it. When this vapour cools it forms tiny drops of water that make up clouds. If the drops become bigger, they may fall as rain.

▼ In an aneroid barometer, a disc shrinks or expands as air pressure changes. This moves the pointer.

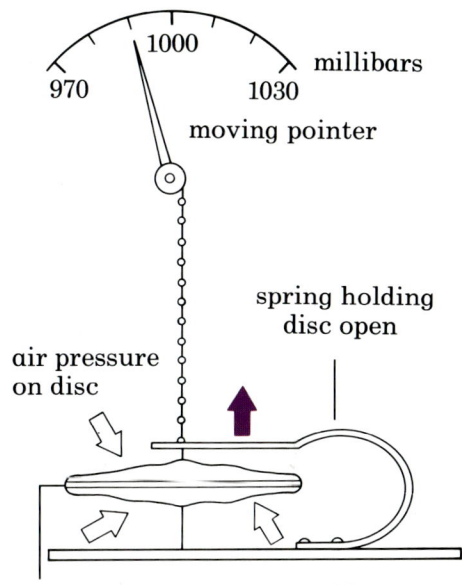

millibars

moving pointer

spring holding disc open

air pressure on disc

disc with little air inside

Did you know?

Air pressure is measured by a **barometer**. One type of barometer is a mercury barometer. It is a column of mercury inside a glass tube which rises and falls with changes in air pressure. Another type is an aneroid barometer (see above). Air pressure is usually measured in millibars (mb).

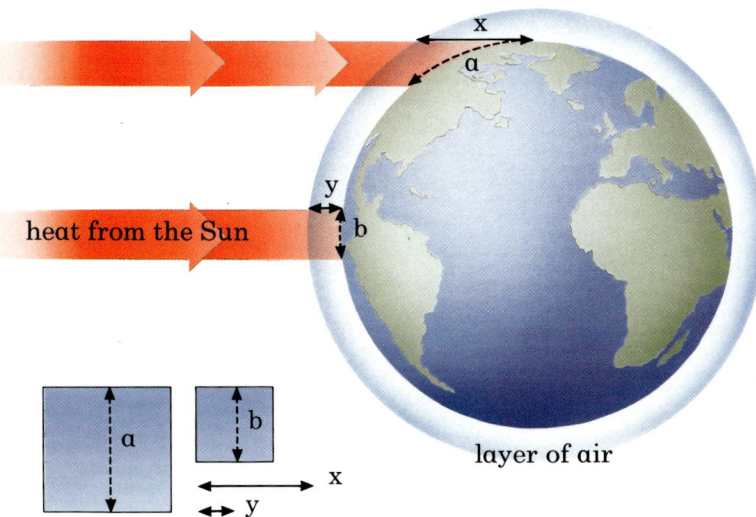

heat from the Sun

layer of air

◄ Showing how the Sun's heat falls over more land (a) and travels through more air (x) at the poles than at the Equator (b), (y).

7

Clouds

Fog and mist

Fog forms when water vapour condenses near the ground. Fog is made of millions of tiny water droplets, like those in a cloud. Fog can make it difficult to see far. Mist forms in the same way as fog, but it is not so thick.

▼ During clear, calm nights, mist can form in valleys. It often lasts well into the morning.

When you boil water, it rapidly turns into a gas called water vapour. This change is called **evaporation**. It also takes place at normal temperatures. Puddles on the ground dry up because of evaporation. When air rises, it often takes vapour with it. As it rises, it cools and the vapour changes back into tiny drops of water. This is called **condensation**. In time, the drops group together to form clouds.

Cloud types

There are ten types of cloud. The most important are cirrus, cumulus and stratus. Cirrus means a curl of hair. Cirrus clouds look like wispy threads

◄ Five of the most common types of cloud. From top to bottom: high, streaky cirrus; patchy, grey-white altocumulus; heavy cumulonimbus (the thunder cloud); cotton-wool-like cumulus; and grey, low-lying stratus, shown here covering the top of the Eiffel Tower.

and float as high as 10,000 metres above the ground. Cumulus means heap. Cumulus clouds appear as great banks in the sky. Stratus means layer and stratus clouds form low grey layers. Alto, which means high, and nimbus, which means rain-bearing, are also used to describe clouds.

The ten cloud types

Cirrus: high, white, wispy, hair-like cloud.
Cirrocumulus: thin sheets of cloud forming ripples or patches.
Cirrostratus: thin, white, misty cloud.
Altocumulus: grey-white cloud in sheets or patches.
Altostratus: grey, streaky cloud that may cover the sky entirely.
Nimbostratus: thick rain or snow cloud, often dark; blots out the Sun.
Stratocumulus: rolling masses of grey or white cloud with dark patches.
Stratus: grey, low-lying cloud; usually produces drizzle; hides hilltops.
Cumulus: separate heaps of cloud which often look like lumps of cotton wool.
Cumulonimbus: heavy, towering thundercloud.

9

▼ A rainbow forms when the Sun shines through raindrops in the sky. The raindrops split up the white sunlight into the seven colours of the rainbow.

Rain, Hail and Snow

Size facts

● The biggest raindrops fall during summer thunderstorms. They can measure 8 mm across.
● The biggest snowflakes can measure up to 50 mm across.
● The biggest and heaviest hailstones ever reported fell in Ohio, USA, in 1981. Some weighed up to 13.6 kg.

Meteorologists use the word **precipitation** to describe all the forms in which water falls to the ground. They list eleven types of precipitation. But most people only talk about three – rain, hail and snow. Precipitation begins by ice particles or tiny water droplets joining together. It can take up to one million droplets to form one raindrop.

Falling to the ground

As the droplets in a cloud grow larger, they become heavy enough to fall to the ground. Ice particles sometimes melt and fall as rain, but if the air is cold they fall as hail or snow. Hailstones are heavy and fall rapidly. Even in summer, they sometimes reach the ground still frozen. Snow is more common in cold winter weather.

▲ Snowflakes form many shapes but they always have six sides or points.

Dew and frost

At night, the Sun no longer warms the ground. Then, grass and other things on the ground may become cool enough for water vapour in the air to condense on them as drops of water. We call these drops dew. If it is very cold, the vapour may condense as drops of ice called frost.

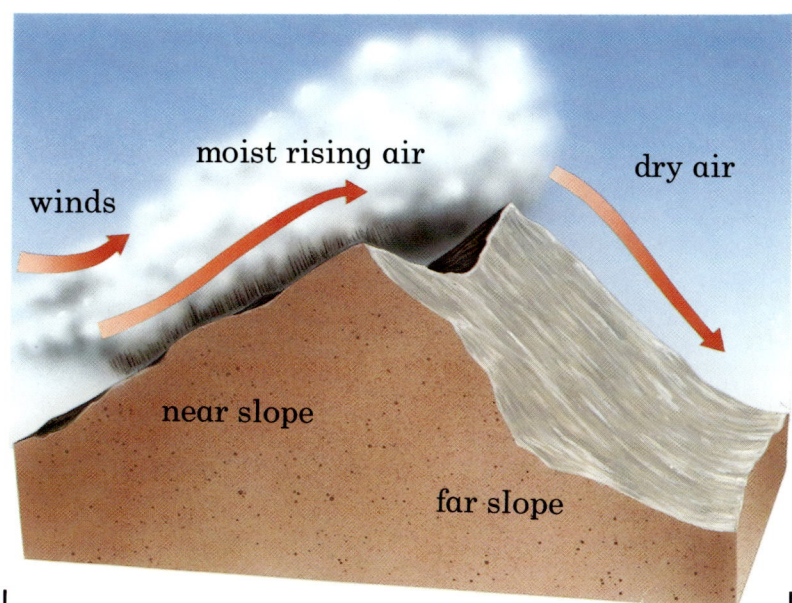

moist rising air

dry air

winds

near slope

far slope

◄ The wind forces moist air to cross mountains. Clouds form and rain falls on the mountains' near side. The far side gets little rain – it is in a rain shadow.

When the wind blows clouds up over mountains, the clouds cool and drop their moisture as rain on the upward slopes of the mountains. Across the mountains it is much drier. This dry area is called a rain shadow.

Did you know?

Rain can seem to fall from a clear sky because the cloud it comes from has already broken up.

Wind, Highs and Lows

▶ This US weather satellite picture shows two lows over western Europe. The lows are the two swirls of cloud over Sweden and the North Sea. These clouds are made by the way winds blow around lows.

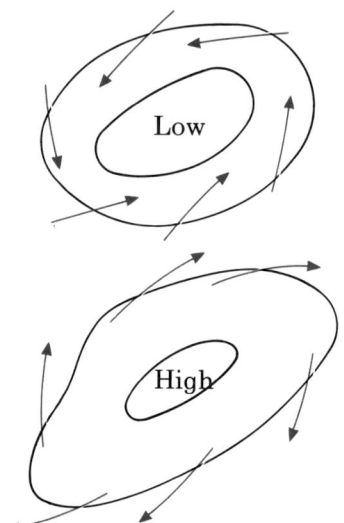

▲ The arrows show how winds blow around a low and slightly inwards (top) and around a high and slightly outwards (bottom).

When air is rising, air pressure at ground level is often low. Winds blow around and inwards to the centre of lower pressure. This centre is called a **low** or a **cyclone**. If the air pressure at ground level is high, the winds

blow around and outwards from the centre. This centre is called a **high** or an **anticyclone**.

Highs and lows bring different

weather. Lows usually bring bad weather. They have heavy clouds and strong winds. Lows bring rain or even storms. Highs have few clouds and light winds. In highs, you can usually expect good, sunny weather.

Changes in the wind

The wind does not blow evenly. When it blows over the bumpy land, it becomes gusty. Gusts of wind can be different even if they are only 100 metres apart. Gusty winds usually change direction. They can veer – change direction clockwise – or they can back – change direction anticlockwise.

Coastal breezes

In coastal areas, the wind often changes direction between day and night. The land heats up during the day so the air above it gets warmer and rises. To take its place, cool air blows inland from over the sea. Sailing boats use this sea breeze to come back to land by day. At night, the land cools and the wind blows gently out to sea.

▼ During the day, warm air rises over land and cool air blows in from the sea (yellow arrow). At night, the sea is warmer than the land so the wind blows in the other direction.

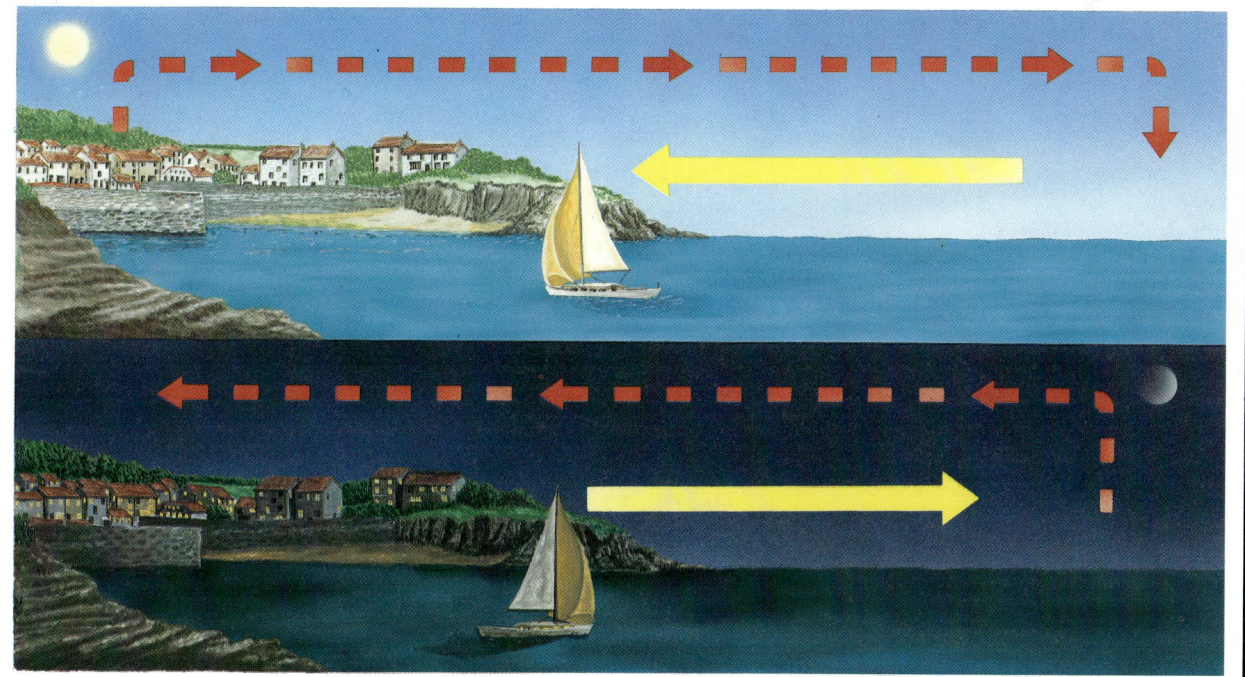

Storms

► A tornado twists across farmland in the USA.

▼ Tropical storm diagram: Rising air (1) sucks in air from below (2). The centre called the 'eye' stays calm (3). Winds spiral out high up (4).

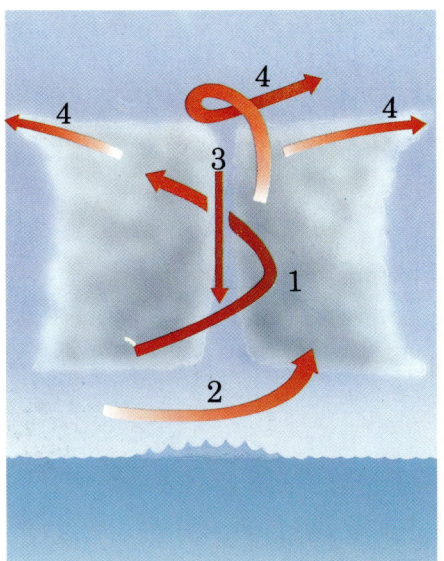

Winds grow strongest when a low develops. Air is sucked into the low near the ground and hurled out of the low right up in the sky. If the low is very big the winds become very strong and a storm blows up.

Tropical storms

The most violent winds occur in tropical storms. These develop over the sea, but they may move over land and do terrible damage. In the Caribbean Sea and the North Atlantic Ocean, these storms are called hurricanes.

Did you know?

The worst tropical storm ever recorded killed a million people in Bangladesh in 1970. The worst tornado killed 689 people in the USA in 1925.

They are called cyclones in the Indian Ocean and typhoons in the North Pacific Ocean. A tropical storm may be hundreds of kilometres across and its winds may blow over 200 km per hour.

Tornadoes

A tornado is a small funnel of wind (about 100 metres across) that twists around at up to 300 km per hour. It can suck up everything in its path – even buildings and cars! Most tornadoes take place over the United States.

Thunderstorms

Thunderstorms develop in towering cumulonimbus clouds. Strong currents of air rush up and down in these clouds. This makes **static electricity** build up in them – just as it does when you brush your hair. After a while, the static electricity produces a huge spark called lightning. This suddenly heats the air, so causing thunder. To work out how far away a thunderstorm is, count the number of seconds between seeing a flash and hearing the thunder. Divide this number by three to get the distance in kilometres.

▼ Lightning hits the CN Tower in Toronto, Canada.

Reporting on the Weather

CHAPTER THREE

THE WEATHER FORECAST

If weather forecasters want to find out what the weather will be like tomorrow, they need to find out about today's weather over a wide area. If the forecasters want to predict further into the future, they will need weather information from a much larger area. To make a forecast for three or four days ahead information is

Country sayings

Country sayings often predict the weather. But they are not very accurate. For example:

Red sky at night,
The shepherd's delight;
Red sky in the morning,
The shepherd's warning.

At night *and* in the morning, a pale red sky with wispy clouds may mean good weather, but a cloudy, dark red sky usually means rain.

▶ An American ground hog. In North America, there is a saying that if a ground hog can see its shadow on 2 February, then winter will last for six more weeks.

needed from around half the world!

The forecasters need to know about wind, air pressure, **humidity**, clouds, rain and snow. This information is gathered by weather stations, ships, weather balloons and human watchers.

Weather systems are moving all over the world. Some move fast and some move slowly, so sometimes they overlap. This makes it almost impossible to predict the weather more than ten days ahead.

▲ A human watcher uses a simple weather station that records temperature and humidity. The cover shades the **thermometers** and lets air in.

▼ A weather ship records changes of temperature, humidity, air pressure and wind at sea.

Collecting Weather Information

Meteorologists use many ways to collect weather information from high above the ground. **Radar scanners** sweep the sky to find out about clouds and rain. They can tell if rain is light or heavy. Weather balloons float high up into the sky, carrying special instruments called sondes. The sondes sample the weather conditions and radio this information back to stations on the ground.

Satellites go highest of all.

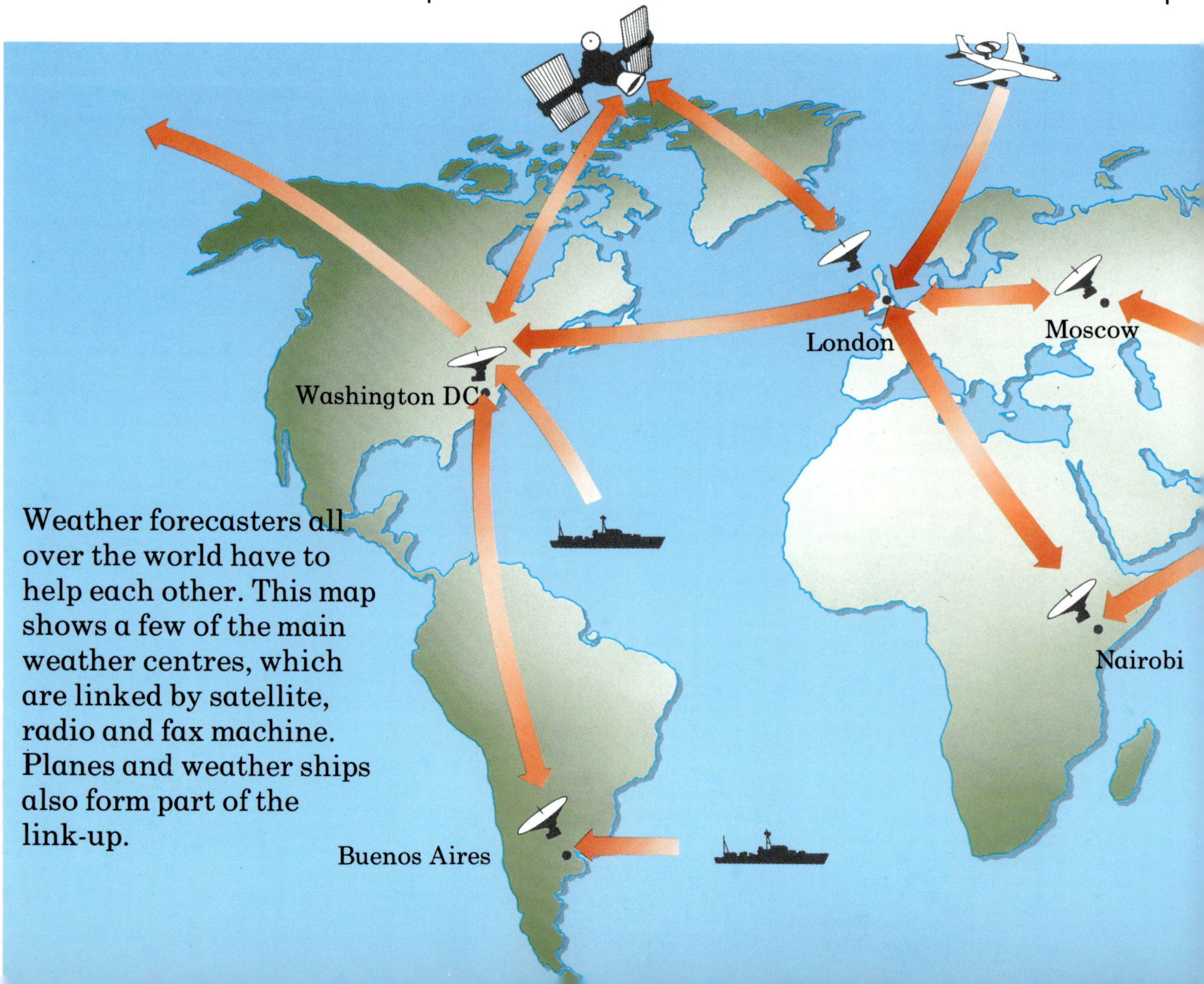

Weather forecasters all over the world have to help each other. This map shows a few of the main weather centres, which are linked by satellite, radio and fax machine. Planes and weather ships also form part of the link-up.

London

Moscow

Washington DC

Nairobi

Buenos Aires

They orbit the Earth and send us pictures of weather systems. You sometimes see these satellite pictures on the television weather forecasts.

Information about weather must be sent quickly from one place to another or it becomes useless. This is because the weather conditions can change so fast. Meteorologists use communication satellites that are linked together to send information across long distances at high speed.

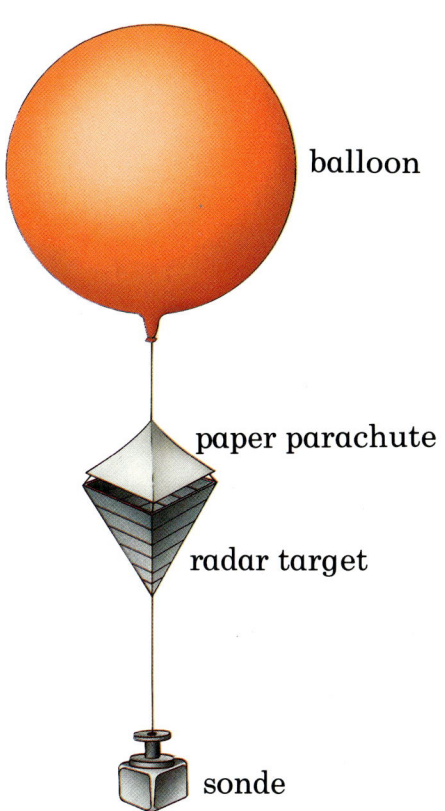

balloon

paper parachute

radar target

sonde

▲ A weather balloon carries a sonde. This measures the weather high above the ground. The balloon's radar target allows radar to track it from the ground. When it gets too high, the balloon bursts and the sonde floats down on its parachute.

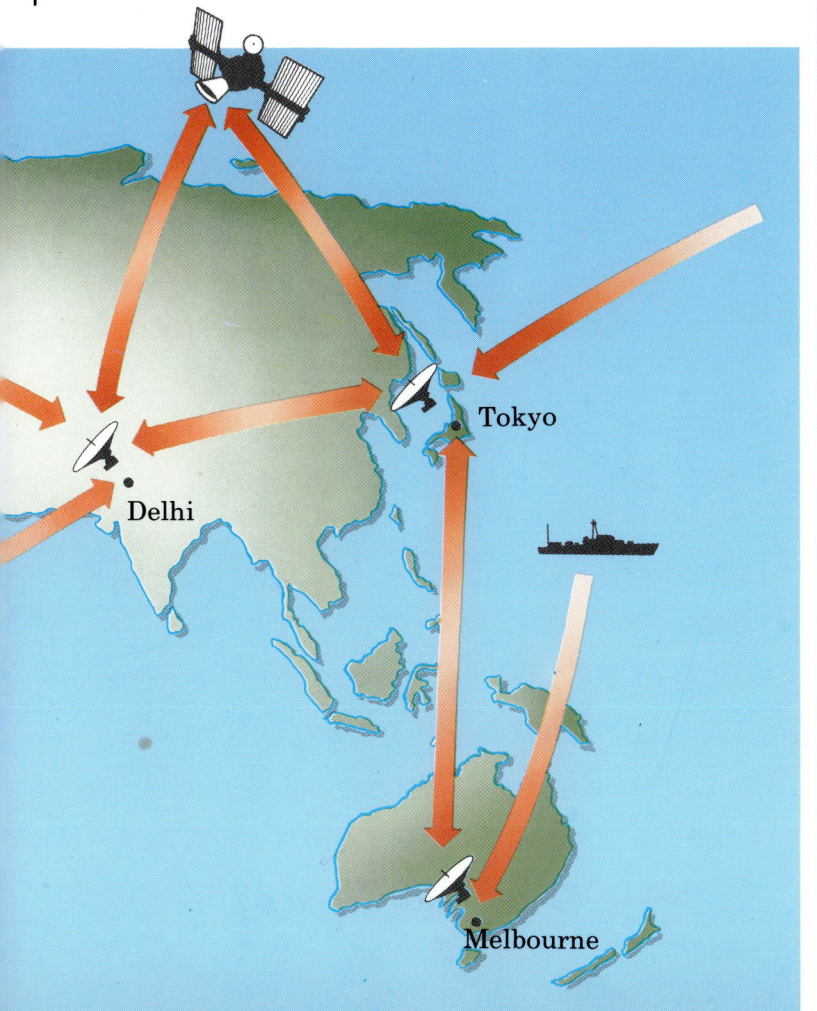

Delhi

Tokyo

Melbourne

Computer link-up

All the major weather centres are linked into a huge computer network. Each centre can send information around the world very quickly.

Putting It All Together

People can work out a weather forecast over a small area for the next 18 hours. Very large computers are needed to make weather forecasts for larger areas or longer periods of time.

Highs and lows are constantly moving about. This changes temperature and wind direction. The computer can work out where the changes will be. It prints them on to a map. Next swirling lines, called **isobars**, are added.

► This chart shows how weather information is collected together to bring you the daily forecast.

▼ Isobars are lines on a weather map that join places with equal air pressure. Iso means 'equal'. The numbers show the air pressure in millibars (mb).

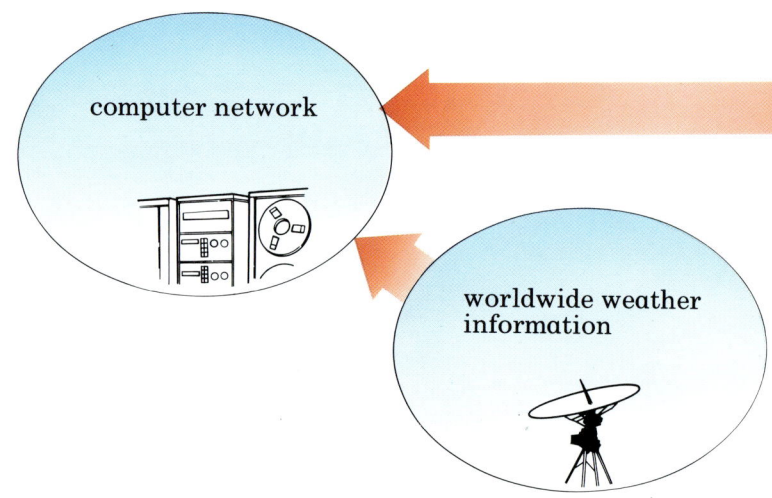

computer network

worldwide weather information

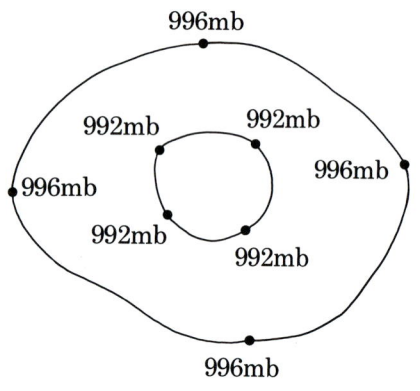

996mb
992mb   992mb
996mb   996mb
992mb
992mb
996mb

These show where the lows and highs are and their shape. By looking at the map and at recent satellite photographs of clouds, the forecaster is able to decide what is likely to happen next.

Weather forecasting is not easy

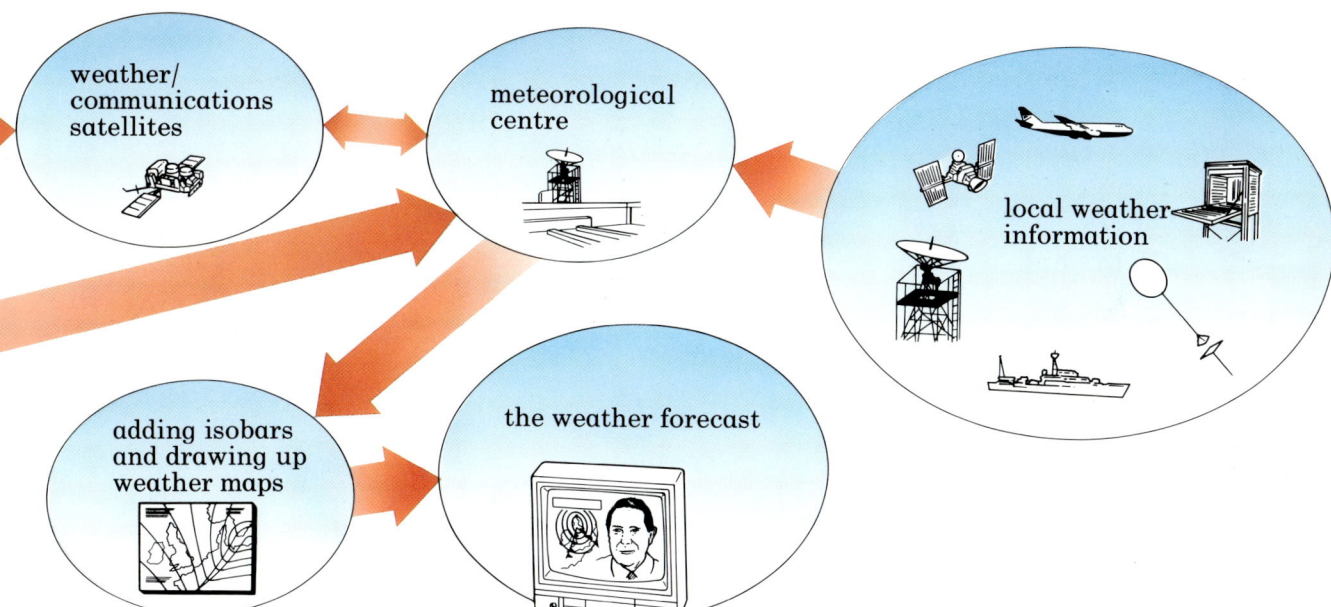

weather/
communications
satellites

meteorological
centre

local weather
information

adding isobars
and drawing up
weather maps

the weather forecast

but predictions are mostly right.
If they are wrong, it is usually
because it is difficult to tell
exactly how fast the weather is
moving. Rain may come earlier or
later than predicted.

▲ Top: a weather
forecaster at work. The
computer screens give him
weather information from
around the world.

Weather Maps

▶ A weather map of north-west Europe with a key to help us read it. In the west, there are clouds, rain and strong winds around a low and its connected **fronts** (see page 27). In the east, a high gives clear skies except where the very light wind helps to form mists.

(see page 27)

A weather map may look complicated but anyone can learn to read one. To find the highs and lows, look at the isobars. Closely-spaced isobars show a low. A low usually brings cloudy weather with wind and rain.

If the isobars are widely spaced, you are probably looking at a high. A high usually brings clear weather and light winds.

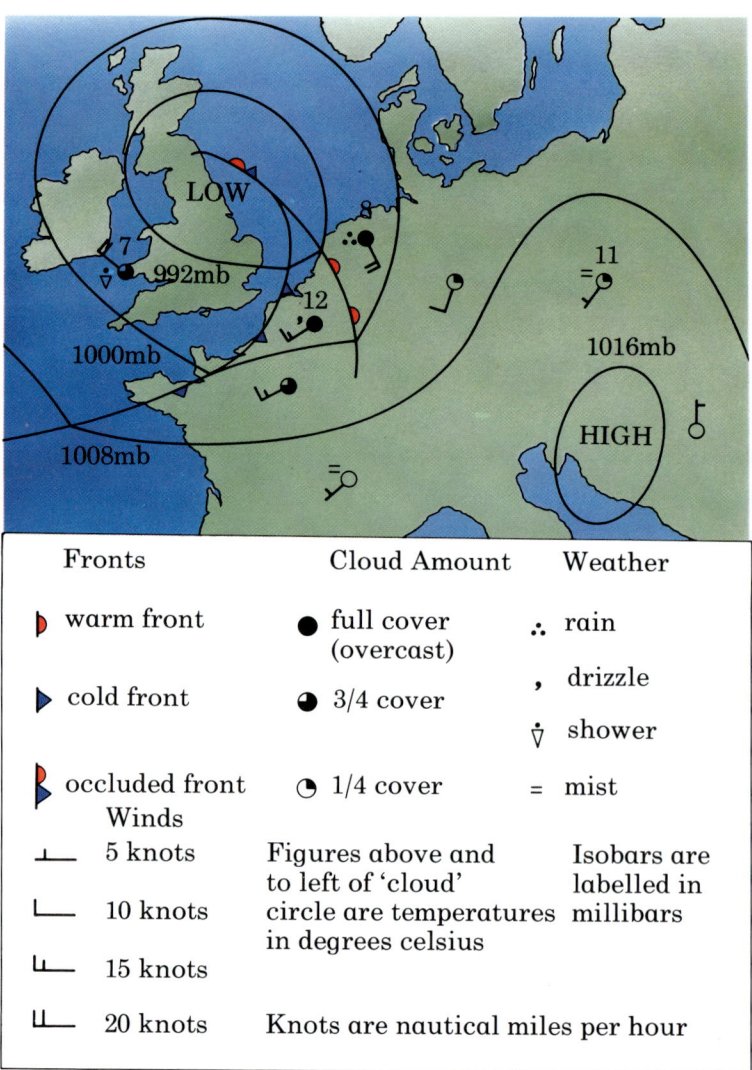

Fronts	Cloud Amount	Weather
warm front	● full cover (overcast)	∴ rain
cold front	◑ 3/4 cover	, drizzle
occluded front	◔ 1/4 cover	∇ shower
Winds		= mist
5 knots	Figures above and to left of 'cloud' circle are temperatures in degrees celsius	Isobars are labelled in millibars
10 knots		
15 knots		
20 knots	Knots are nautical miles per hour	

Who uses forecasts?

Some people particularly need detailed weather forecasts. For example, farmers need to know when weather conditions might help the spread of plant diseases. Gas and electricity suppliers need to know if it will be cold so they can supply more power for heating homes and offices.

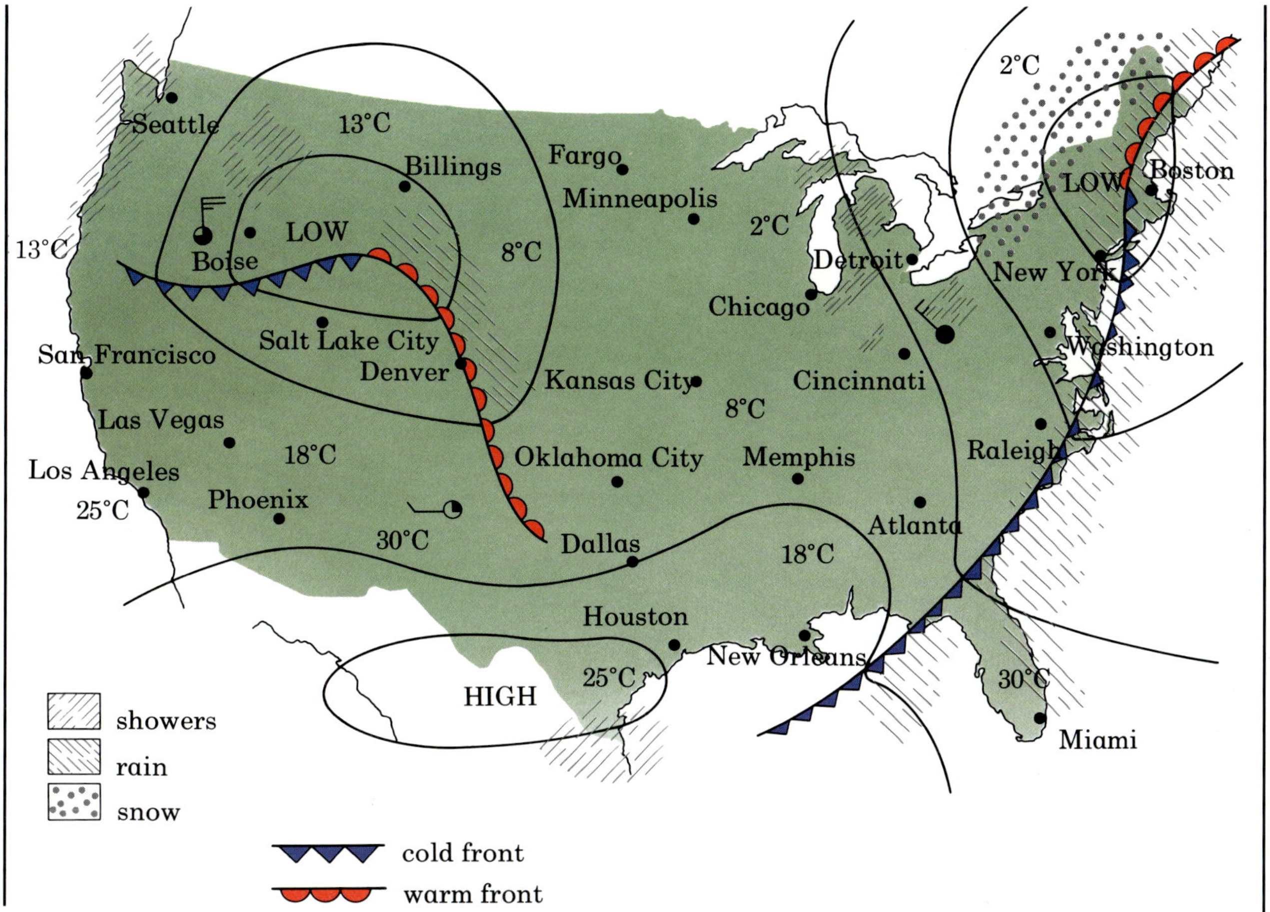

A weather map showing the United States with temperatures and weather fronts.

Seattle
13°C
Billings
Fargo
Minneapolis
2°C
LOW
Boise
13°C
8°C
Detroit
Chicago
LOW Boston
New York
San Francisco
Salt Lake City
Denver
Washington
Kansas City
Cincinnati
8°C
Las Vegas
Los Angeles
18°C
Oklahoma City
Memphis
Raleigh
25°C
Phoenix
30°C
Dallas
18°C
Atlanta
Houston
25°C
New Orleans
30°C
Miami
HIGH
2°C

showers
rain
snow
cold front
warm front

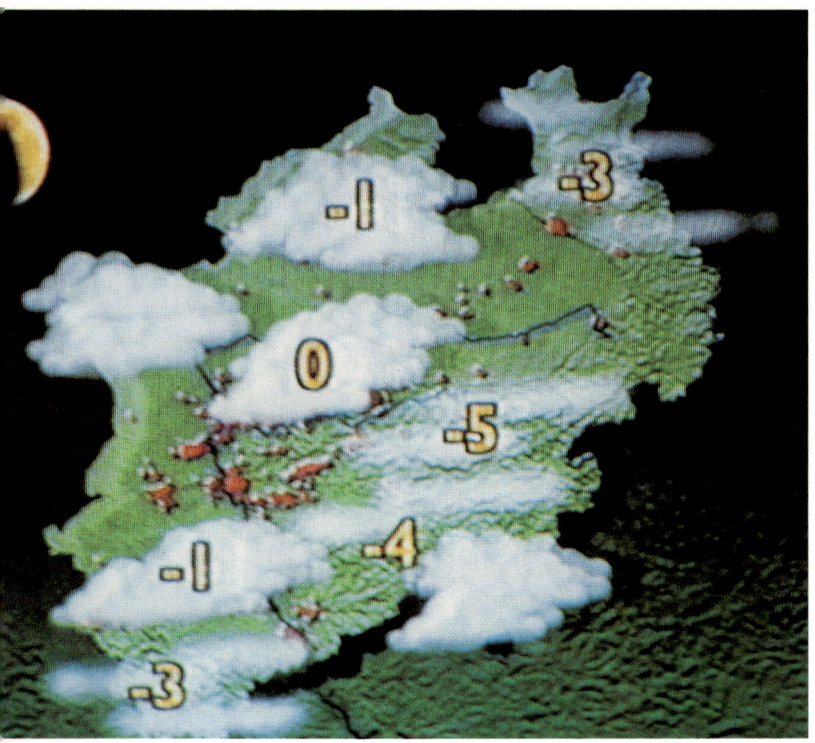

▲ A weather map of the
United States for a day in
April. Over the east coast,
there is rain connected
with a cold front. Further
north-east, it is cold and
there is snow caused by a
low with a warm front. In
the south there is a high
which gives very warm
temperatures. In the
north-west, there is
another low and it is cool
and rainy.

◄ TV forecasters explain
their predictions with
simple weather maps like
this one from Germany.

The World's Climates

The Climates

Icecap: always frozen.

Polar: cold and dry.

Subarctic: cold winters and short cool summers.

Steppe: great changes from hot to cold; dry.

Highlands: colder areas.

Continental moist: cold winters, warm summers.

Oceanic moist: mild winters, warmer summers.

Desert: very dry; hot by day and cold by night.

Subtropical dry summer: wet winters, dry summers.

Subtropical moist: cool winters, hot summers.

Tropical wet and dry: Hot; dry and wet seasons.

Tropical wet: hot and wet.

CHAPTER FOUR

CLIMATE

Climate controls the kinds of plants and animals that live in a certain area. It also affects the way people live, such as how they dress. In a hot climate people often wear light, cotton clothes but, in a cold climate, they wear heavy, woolly clothes.

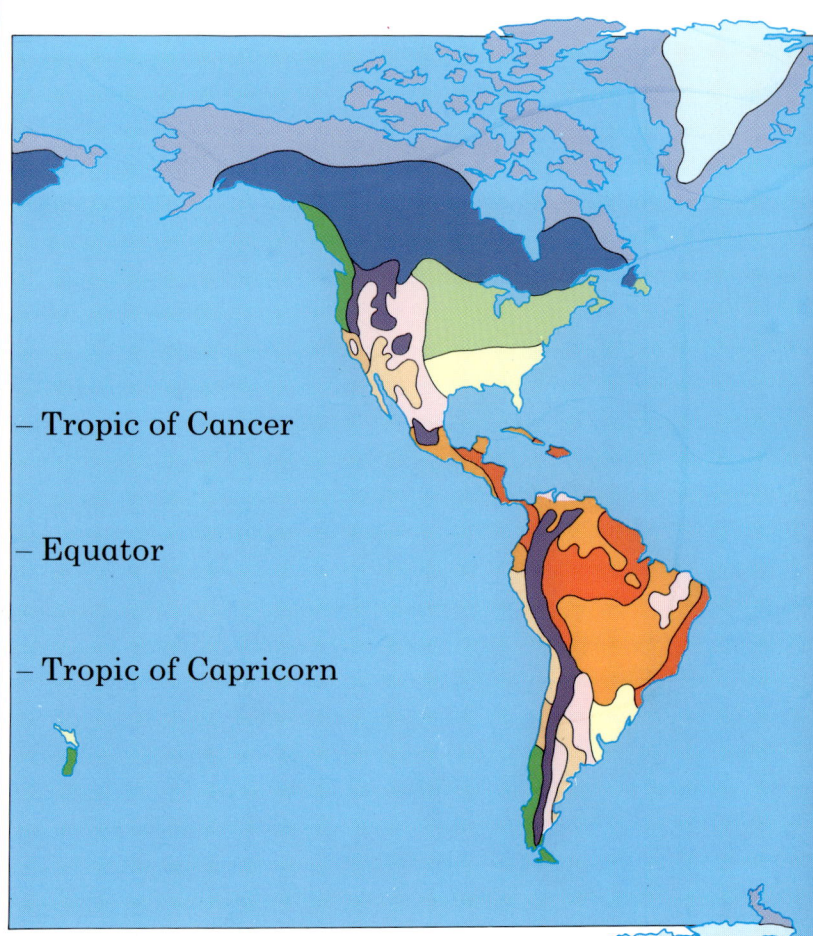

– Tropic of Cancer

– Equator

– Tropic of Capricorn

Different climates

Climatologists have found there are 12 different types of climate. They range from cold and dry at the polar ice caps to hot and wet near the Equator. Each climate type has some differences within it. For example, although all of Britain is in the same climate type, the Scottish Highlands are usually colder than south-west England. Also, the West of Britain usually has more rain than the East of the country.

▲ Mount Kenya lies near the Equator, but it is always capped with snow. Below it are warm grasslands. This shows how there can be differences within one climate area.

Protective skin colour

Over many thousands of years in hot climates, such as in Africa and Australia, people's skin has become dark. This helps protect them from the Sun's harmful rays.

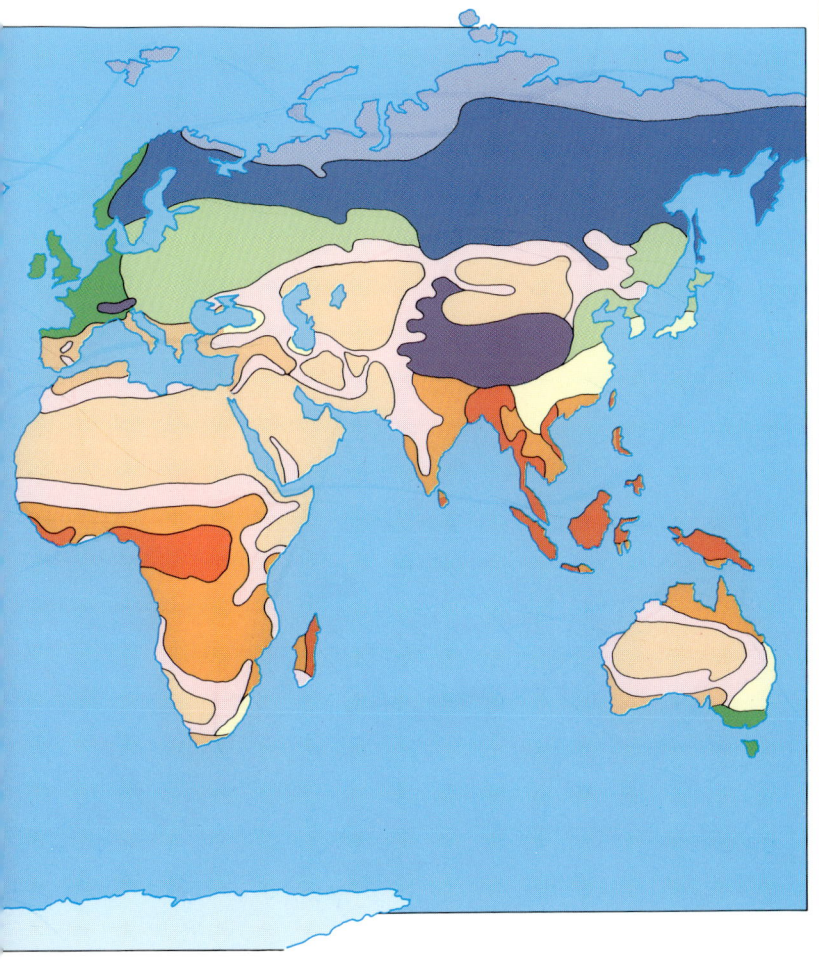

◄ This map shows the world's climate areas. The key is on the page opposite. The climate of Britain and western Europe is oceanic moist. There are only a few other areas in the world with this climate.

Water and Air

▼ This map shows the world's main warm and cold ocean currents. Cold deep polar currents tend to move towards the Equator while warm surface currents move away from it.

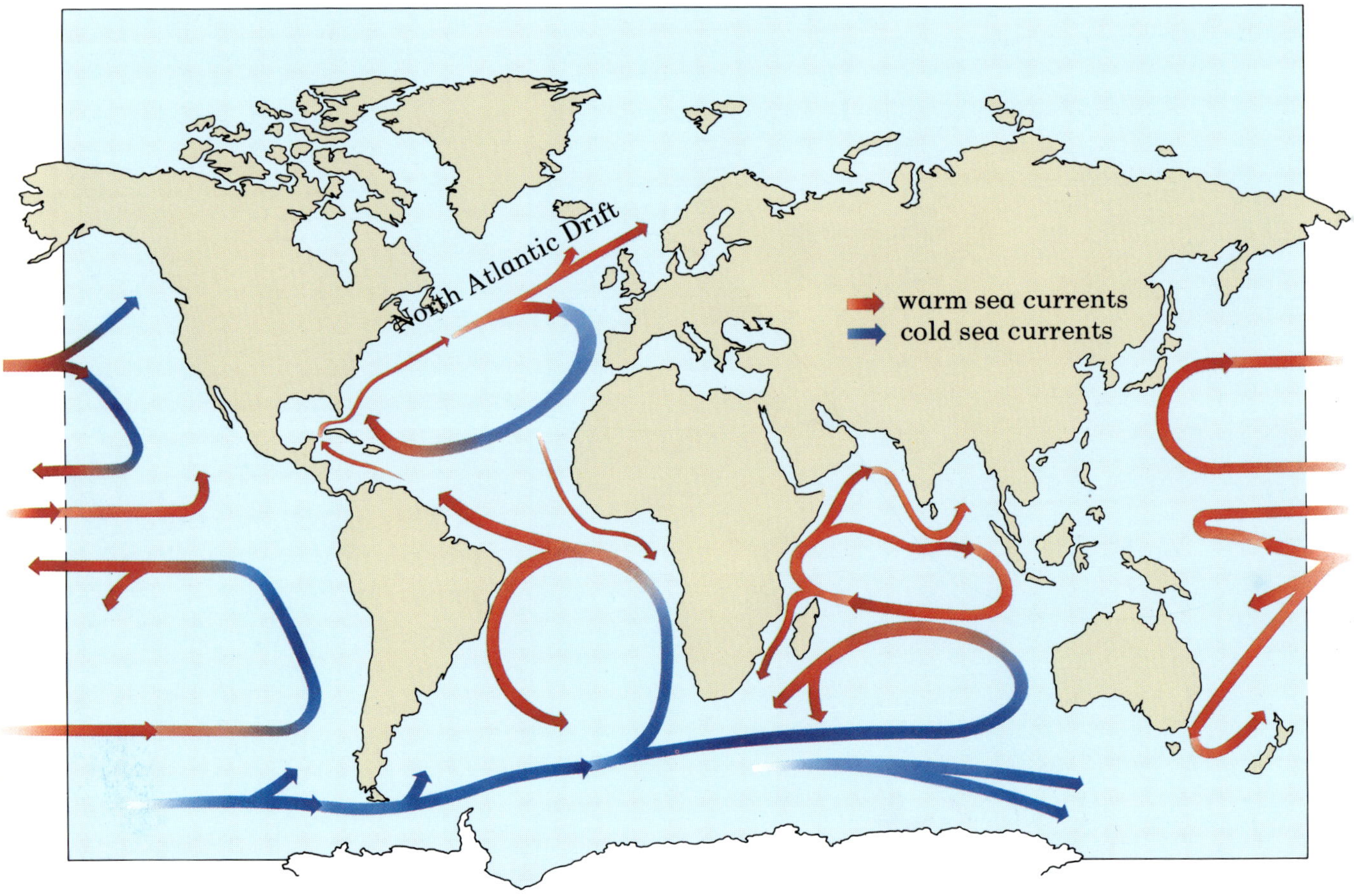

The sea heats up and cools down more slowly than the land. As a result, the sea stays at a more steady temperature. This affects the climates of coastal areas. They have fewer changes in temperature than inland areas.

Coastal areas are also affected by the flow of water currents around the sea. Currents can be warm or cold. The North Atlantic Drift is a warm current that flows towards northern Europe. It warms the western coasts of Britain and Norway.

North Atlantic Drift

→ warm sea currents
→ cold sea currents

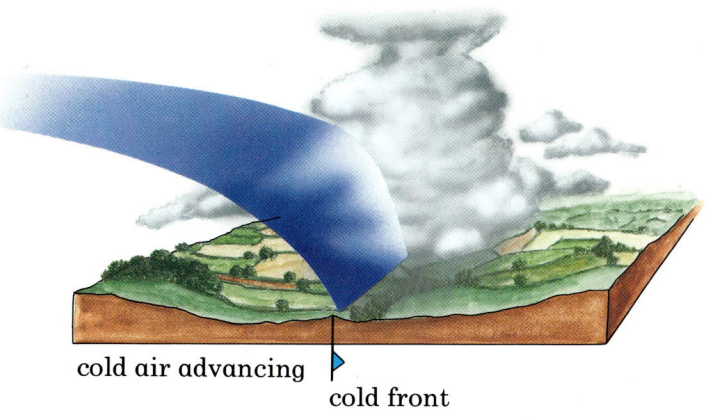

cold air advancing

cold front

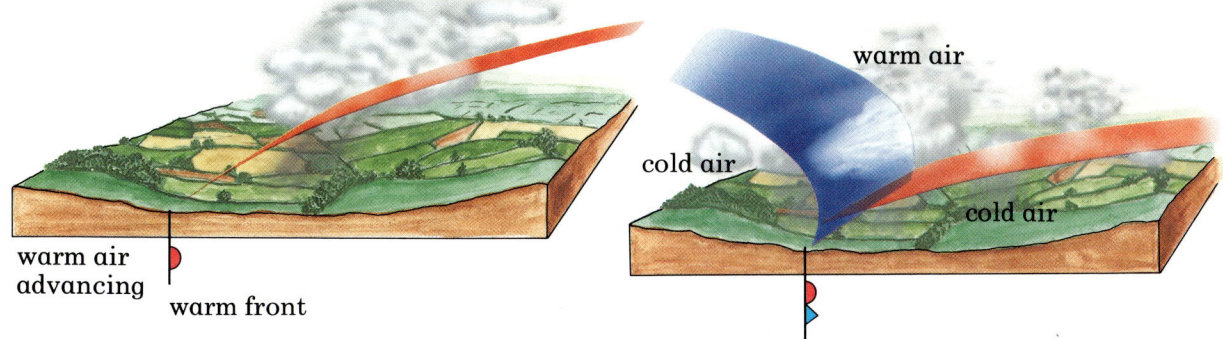

warm air advancing

warm front

warm air

cold air

cold air

occluded front

Which direction?

When we talk about the direction of an ocean current, we mean the direction *towards* which the current flows. So a southerly current flows from north to south.

Air masses

An **air mass** is a large body of air that moves around the world. It can be hot or cold depending on where it comes from. An air mass that comes from the Equator will be warm. An air mass from the poles will be cold.

Where an air mass catches up with another one, there is a boundary at ground level which is called a **front**. Warmer air catching up with cold air gives a warm front. Colder air meeting warm air gives a cold front. If warm air gets caught between two colder air masses, there is an **occluded front**.

▲ Three types of front, the weather they usually bring and the symbols used to show them on weather maps. A cold front brings rain followed by clear skies. A warm front brings low clouds, with rain or snow. Occluded fronts may bring rain, but this is harder to predict.

El Niño

El Niño is a warm sea current that sometimes flows in the Pacific. It blocks the usual cold sea currents along the west coast of South America. As a result, fish move away so people cannot catch as many as usual.

27

The World's Winds

▶ The world's major wind areas. The doldrums and the horse latitudes are calm areas but they do sometimes have storms.

▲ An anemometer measures wind speeds. This one is at the Jodrell Bank Observatory in northern England.

Often winds blow for a few days at a time from any direction. But in some areas of the world there are winds that blow most of the time from the same direction. They are called **prevailing winds**.

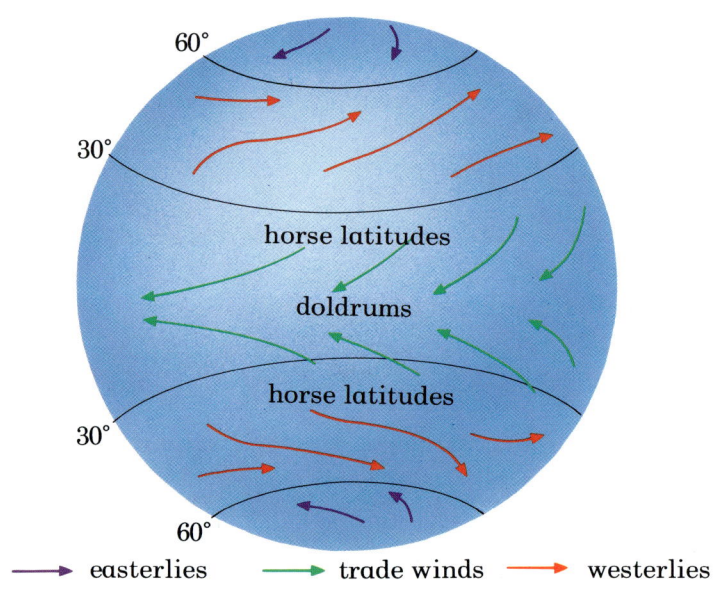

easterlies   trade winds   westerlies

Around the Equator there is little wind. This area is known as the doldrums. Either side of this, there are two areas of winds called the trade winds. They blow towards the Equator and slightly from the east.

Moving further from the Equator, after the trade winds, there comes two areas of calm called the horse latitudes. Next, there are areas of westerlies, winds from the west. Finally,

◀ Strong prevailing winds blowing from the right made these trees grow into a permanent bend.

close to the poles, there are easterlies, winds from the east.

Measuring the wind

An **anemometer** is a special instrument that is used to measure how fast the wind is blowing.

Which direction?

The wind directions we are given tell us where the wind is coming *from*. So a westerly wind blows from the west.

▲ Clouds in a jet stream over Egypt and the Red Sea photographed from a US spacecraft.

The Beaufort Wind Force Scale

Wind speed on land is given in force numbers from 0 to 12.

No.	Name	Speed (km/h)	Effect
0	Calm	Under 1	Smoke goes straight up
1	Light air	1-5	Smoke shows wind
2	Light breeze	6-11	Wind felt on face
3	Gentle breeze	12-19	Leaves rustle
4	Moderate breeze	20-28	Dust and small tree branches move
5	Fresh breeze	29-38	Flags flap
6	Strong breeze	39-49	Large branches sway
7	Moderate gale	50-61	Whole trees sway
8	Fresh gale	62-74	Walking into the wind is difficult
9	Strong gale	75-88	Branches break off; tiles blown off roofs
10	Whole gale	89-102	Trees fall; bad damage
11	Storm	103-117	Very widespread damage
12	Hurricane	over 117	Buildings wrecked

Jet streams

Jet streams are currents of air very high in the sky. They travel at speeds up to 400 km per hour. They can affect the speed of a plane flying near or in them.

Some jet streams blow all the time. Others happen near fronts and lows. Fast-moving, high cloud is probably in a jet stream and means the weather may soon change.

What Makes the Seasons?

The Earth makes one turn every 24 hours. When a place faces the Sun, it has day. When it turns away from the Sun, it has night.

While the Earth turns, it also slowly moves along a path around the Sun. It goes round this path once a year. During this year, we have the seasons: winter, spring, summer and autumn.

The seasons change because the Earth does not turn at an upright angle to its path around the Sun. It is always tilted.

This means that one half of the Earth gets more sunlight than the other. This half has summer while the other half has winter. But as the Earth moves along its path, the half that was tilted towards

▼ ► The changing seasons affect plant life. The left-hand photograph was taken in New England, USA, in summer. The right-hand photograph is the same scene in autumn.

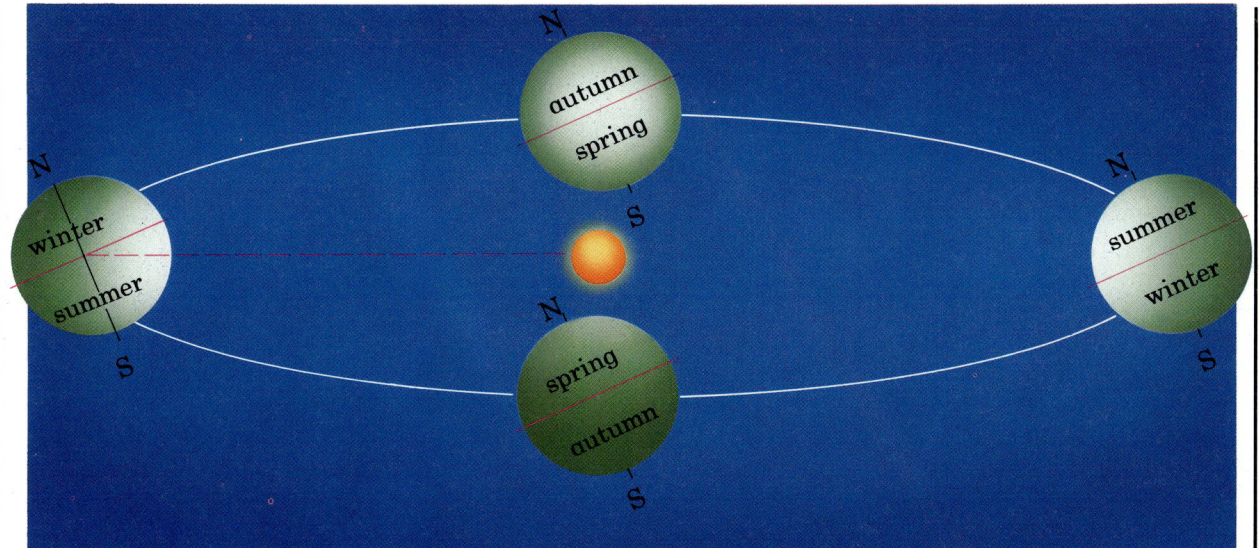

the Sun slowly moves away. More sunlight now falls on the other half and it has summer.

During this change between winter and summer, the half that is gaining sunlight begins to warm up and has spring; the half that is losing sunlight begins to cool down and has autumn.

▲ Each day, the Earth turns around a line that passes through the North (N) and South (S) Poles. The diagram shows how this line is tilted at an angle to the Earth's path around the Sun. As a result, different areas get more sunshine during the year and the seasons change.

What Makes a Climate?

Climates are caused by the Sun heating the Earth by day. At times, such as night, the Earth will lose some of this heat. The amount of heat the Earth gains or loses changes from place to place. The overall amount of heat that a place keeps is called the **radiation balance**.

Gains and losses of heat

The radiation balance changes around the Earth for many reasons. The Sun's heat is strongest at the Equator. As you move towards the poles, this heat gets weaker and weaker.

▼ A mountain pass photographed on both sides on the same day in late summer. Left: the north-facing slope is snow-covered. Right: the south-facing slope is clear of snow because it has a warmer climate.

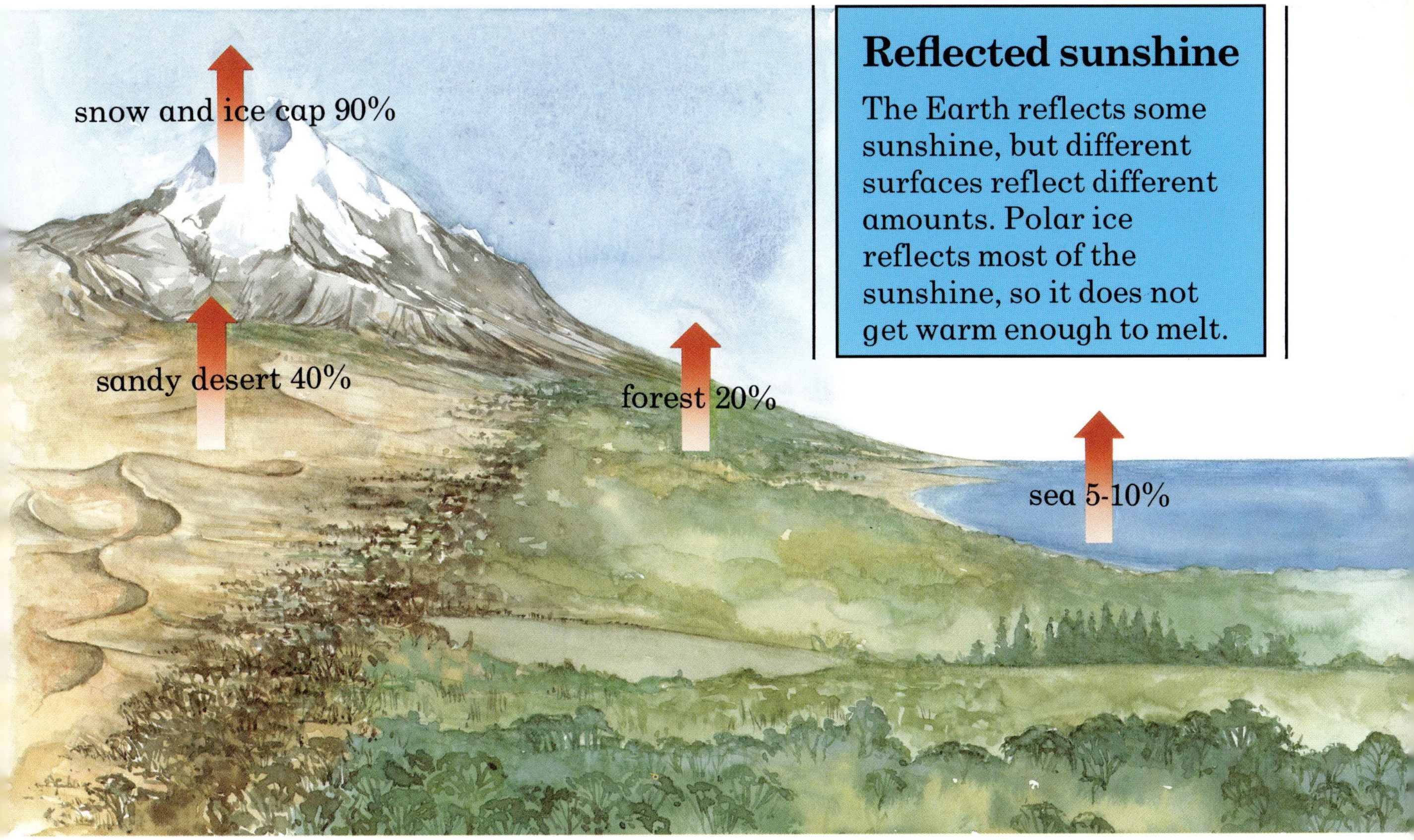
snow and ice cap 90%
sandy desert 40%
forest 20%
sea 5-10%

Reflected sunshine

The Earth reflects some sunshine, but different surfaces reflect different amounts. Polar ice reflects most of the sunshine, so it does not get warm enough to melt.

In the northern half of the world, land that slopes southwards gains more of the Sun's heat. In the world's southern half, land sloping northwards is warmer. Crops grow well on these warmer slopes.

The Sun's heat is also stronger where the sky is clear. Clouds or dirt in the air stop its heat reaching the Earth.

Land loses heat quickly but the sea keeps heat. This makes many coastal climates warmer than those much further inland.

▲ Percentage amounts of the sunshine that some surfaces reflect.

▼A solar power station makes electricity using the sun's heat.

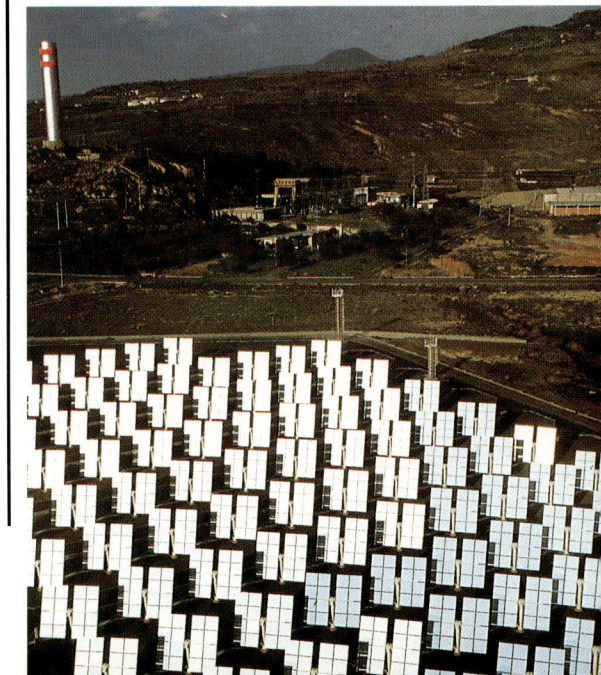

The Changing Sun

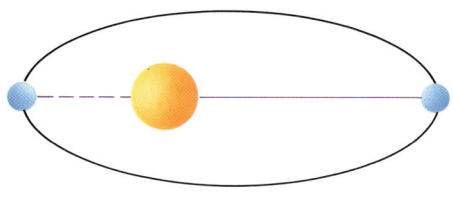

- - - nearest distance
——— furthest distance

▲ This diagram shows the Earth's ellipse-shaped path around the Sun and its nearest and furthest distances from the Sun.

▶ This photograph, taken from space, shows the ever-changing surface of the Sun. It is a huge ball of burning gases. The glowing loop of gas on the left reached a temperature of 20,000°C. Water boils at only 100°C!

The Earth's path around the Sun is not a perfect circle. It is an ellipse, a shape like a squashed circle. The Sun is not in the middle of the ellipse but slightly towards one end of it. So at times the Earth is nearer the Sun than at others. The changing distances affect the Earth's climate.

The Sun is a huge ball of burning gases. It is always changing so the amount of heat it gives out may change, too.

Spots on the Sun

Sunspots are one way we can see the Sun is changing. They are dark patches that appear on the Sun's surface. Every few years they become more common.

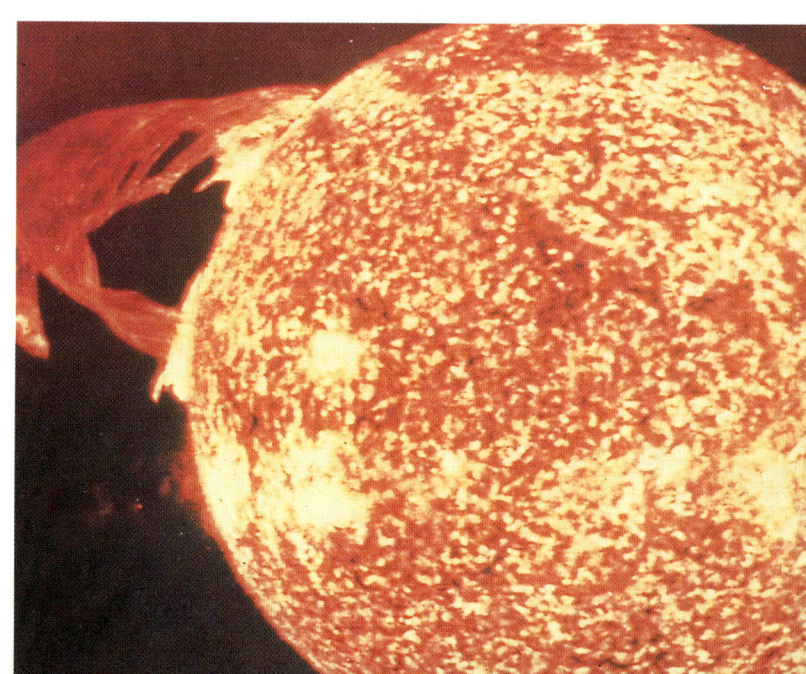

◄ The aurora borealis, or Northern Lights, seen in the Alaskan sky. These beautiful lights are made by tiny particles from the Sun mixing with the air very high – between 100 km and 1,000 km – above the ground.

Sunspot facts

● Sunspots are dark patches which appear from time to time on the Sun's surface.
● When there are a lot of sunspots, the aurora borealis may appear in the northern sky.
● Sunspot activity can interfere with TV and radio transmissions.
Warning: Never look at the Sun. It can blind you. Even wearing dark glasses or looking through smoked glass would not save your sight.

Some scientists think that a large number of sunspots is usually followed by less rain on Earth, but they are not sure yet why this happens. Every 90 and 200 years, the number of sunspots gets much bigger. This can cause a change in climate. We need to study the Sun to learn how it may affect our climate.

Volcanoes

▲ A volcano erupting and throwing up a huge cloud of ash, gas and dust. Hot lava – melted rock – pours down its sides.

▼ This huge crater in Australia is thought to have been made by a meteorite striking the Earth millions of years ago.

A near miss

Many rocky masses called asteroids go round the Sun. In 1937 one of them came close to hitting the Earth. It was over 1.6 kilometres across – imagine the huge crater it might have made!

When a volcano erupts, it shoots up gas and ash into the sky. The ash is very fine and makes a huge hazy cloud. In 1835, the volcano Cosigüina, in Central America, erupted and threw out 20 cubic kilometres of ash. Imagine how big a cloud it made!

The clouds made by volcanoes block out the Sun's heat. Experts think this can cool the climate for a while.

Meteorites

A **meteorite** is a mass of stone or metal that falls to Earth from space. Millions of years ago, huge meteorites made even bigger dust clouds than volcanoes. Some scientists think that one of these dust clouds blocked out the Sun for several years at the time of the **dinosaurs**. This made a big change to the climate, which killed many of the dinosaurs.

◄ The British artist Joseph Turner (1775-1851) was famous for his beautiful paintings of sunsets, such as this.

Turner sunsets

Turner painted many sunset scenes shortly after Cosigüina erupted in 1835. Light shining through dust from the eruption may have caused these colourful sunsets.

Climate and Plants

coniferous forest

Mediterranean scrub

temperate broadleaved forest

tropical rain forest

grassland

semi-desert

desert

tundra and alpine

ice desert

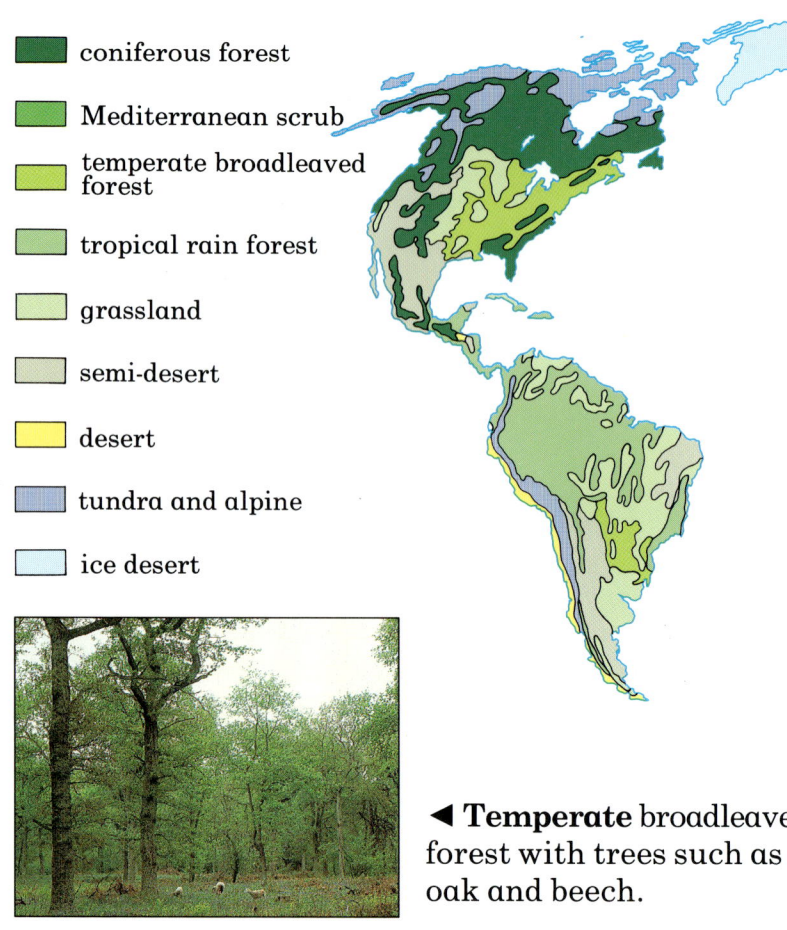

▲ Tundra and alpine plants, such as mosses.

▼ Coniferous forests of fir trees grow in cool areas.

▼ Tropical rain forest grows in hot, wet areas.

◄ **Temperate** broadleaved forest with trees such as oak and beech.

Plants need water, sunlight and some warmth to grow. These needs are controlled by climate, so the plants that grow in an area are ruled by that area's climate.

Around the poles, the climate is so cold that very few plants can grow. This area is called an ice desert.

As you move out of the ice deserts, you find an area called tundra. It is still cold here. No trees can grow but there are little plants, such as mosses, and plants

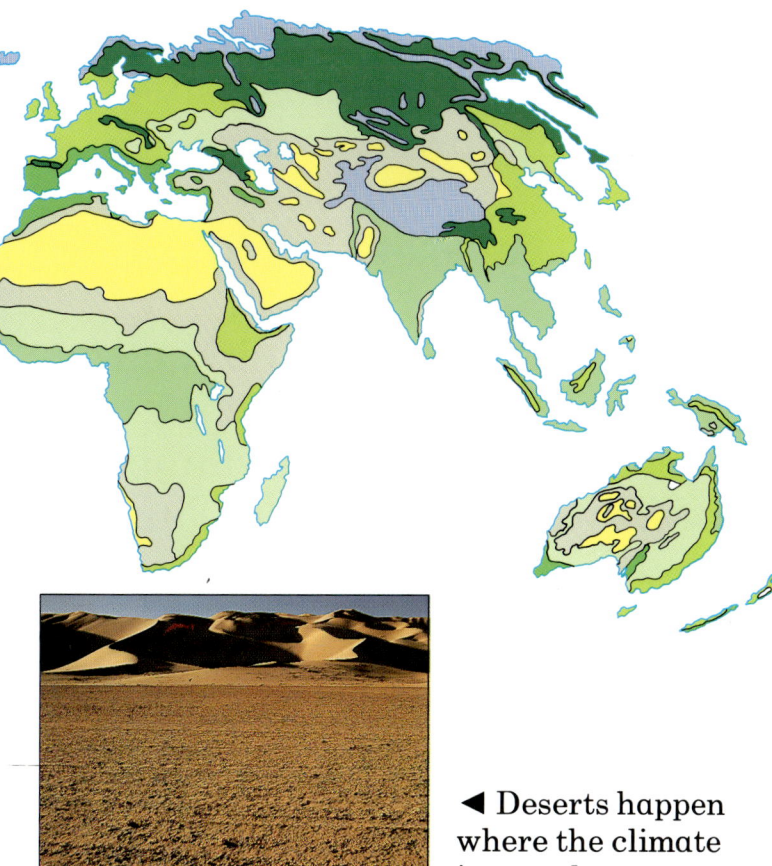

▲ An ice desert is so cold that little can grow.

◄ Deserts happen where the climate is very dry.

▲ Grassland happens where few trees grow.

that grow and flower quickly in the short summers.

Around the Equator, in the areas we call the tropics, it is very hot and wet all year round. Plants love this climate. They grow in huge **rain forests** which contain more types of plant than any other area in the world.

Between the tropics and the poles are plant areas such as desert, grassland and fir forests. You can see pictures of them on these two pages.

▲ Semi-desert has tough plants such as **cacti**.

▲ Mediterranean scrub has dense, woody shrubs.

Climate and Animals

▼ The North African jerboa, or desert rat, lives in a burrow under the ground to protect itself from the hot desert sun. It comes out to hunt for food in the cool nights.

Like plants, animals are affected by climate. In hot places, such as deserts, some animals dig burrows where they stay all day. They only come out at night, when it is cooler.

In cold places, animals such as bears have thick fur. The fur of some animals, such as ermines, turn white in the winter. This helps them hide in the snow. Other animals go into a deep sleep during the winter months. This is called hibernation.

Seasonal travellers

As the seasons change, some

animals travel to places where the season is right for them. In winter, many European birds fly south to Africa where the weather is warmer. But, in the spring, they fly back to Europe as it then has a good food supply.

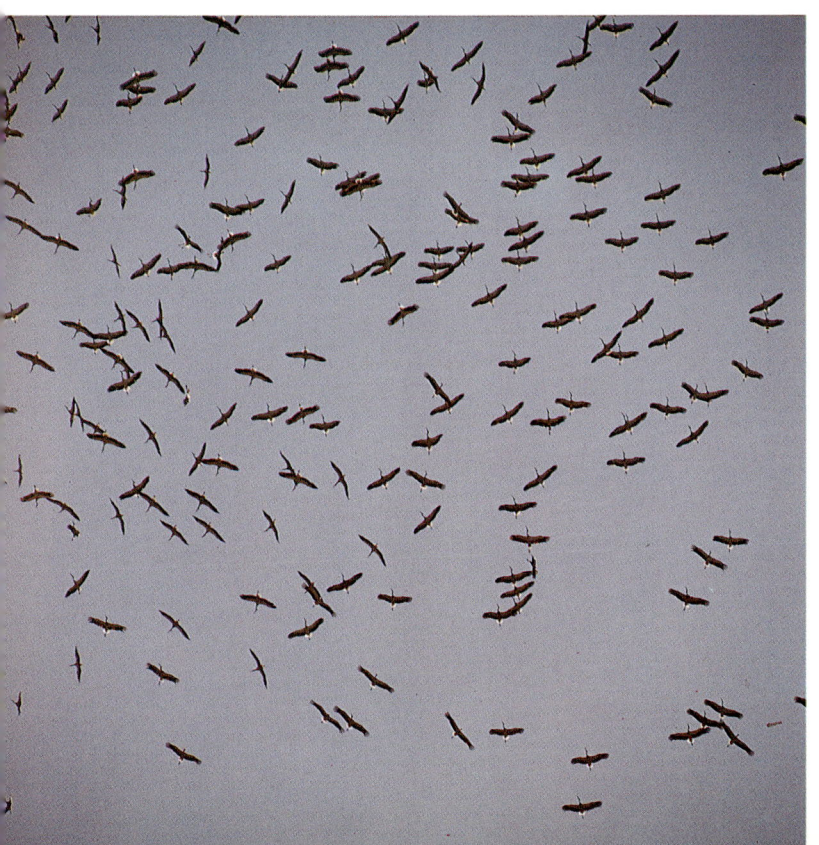

◄ These camels are well suited to life in the desert. The humps on their backs store fat so they can go for days without food or water.

▲ The top picture shows an ermine with its summer coat. The lower one shows it with its white winter coat.
▼ This dormouse will hibernate all winter.

◄ White storks gather together in Africa in spring. They are getting ready to fly to Europe.

Studying Climate Changes

▲ A nilometer on the River Nile at Aswan.

Old instruments

The thermometer was invented in 1592, the barometer in 1644 and rain and wind gauges in the 1600s. But an older and simpler instrument was invented thousands of years ago in Egypt called a nilometer. This measured the level of water in the River Nile. Some still exist today.

CHAPTER FIVE

CHANGING CLIMATES

Over hundreds of years, climates slowly change. We can see this going on today. Since the 1960s, rains that usually fall each year in certain parts of Africa have not arrived. Without the rains, crops have not grown and people in those areas have starved.

Scientists try to understand why such changes happen. They do this by looking at how climates have changed in the past.

Clues to past climates

Scientists have kept weather records for about 300 years. To go further back in time, they find out about the weather from old books, letters and diaries. Nature also gives them clues. A new ring of wood grows in a tree trunk each year. If a year is wet then the tree ring is fat, but if it is dry the ring is thin. Scientists look at old tree trunks to see how much rain fell while the tree was alive.

Some sea creatures flourish in cool water, others in warm. Their remains, found deep in the sea bed, show us what the climate was like millions of years ago.

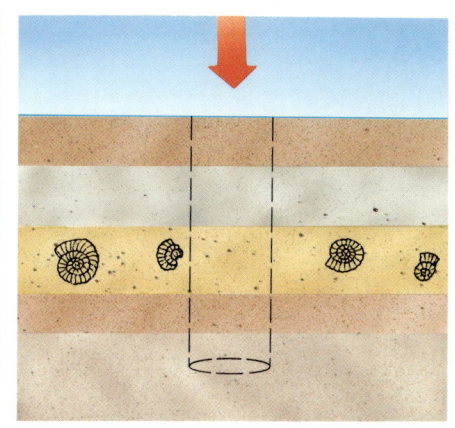

▲ Cylinder-shaped samples are taken of the layers of mud and rock at the bottom of the sea. The layers formed millions of years ago. Scientists can find out about ancient climates from the plant and animal remains found in them.

▼ The rings in this tree stump give us an idea of how much rain fell the year they grew.

◄ This land in western India has become like a desert because the yearly rains have not come. Only four years ago crops grew here.

Ice Ages

In the past 1,000 million years, there have been times when huge areas of the Earth were covered by thick sheets of ice. These times are called ice ages. Today, ice sheets cover about a tenth of the Earth's surface. But during an ice age, ice covered roughly a quarter of it.

Glacials

Ice ages are also called **glacials**. A glacial lasts between 40,000 and 60,000 years. The warmer times between glacials are called **interglacials**. These last between 10,000 and 40,000 years.

We are in an interglacial now which began about 10,000 years

The clues

Clues to when ice ages took place are found in layers of rock which were made millions of years ago. Some layers contain plant remains while other layers do not.

These empty layers were probably made during an ice age, when it was too cold for plants to grow.

▶ The grey colour on this map shows the areas covered by ice during the last Ice Age. You can see that ice covered most of the British Isles.

◀ This valley in the Lake District in north-west England was made during the last Ice Age. Its U-shape was carved out by a huge, slow-moving river of ice called a glacier.

ago. During the last Ice Age, Northern Europe, Siberia and North America had a thick cap of ice. At times, so much water was frozen in the ice cap that the level of the oceans dropped by 100 metres. Britain and Europe were joined by dry land.

▼ A glacier of today in the Swiss Alps. These slow-moving rivers of ice were very common during an ice age.

Climate in Early Times

Where early people went and what they did tells us about the climates they lived in. In Spain and southern France near the end of the last Ice Age, people painted pictures in caves of the animals they hunted, such as mammoths. Mammoths lived in cold areas, so the climate in France and Spain at that time must have been much cooler than it is now.

▶ This map shows the areas in the Middle East where wild wheat grew and the area known as the Fertile Crescent, where people first farmed this wheat.

Radiocarbon dating

All living things have a substance called **radiocarbon** in them. After they die, the radiocarbon decays at a constant rate. Scientists measure the amount of radiocarbon that is left in animal and plant remains, such as bones or wood. This process, called radiocarbon dating, tells them how old the remains are. It can date objects up to 50,000 years old.

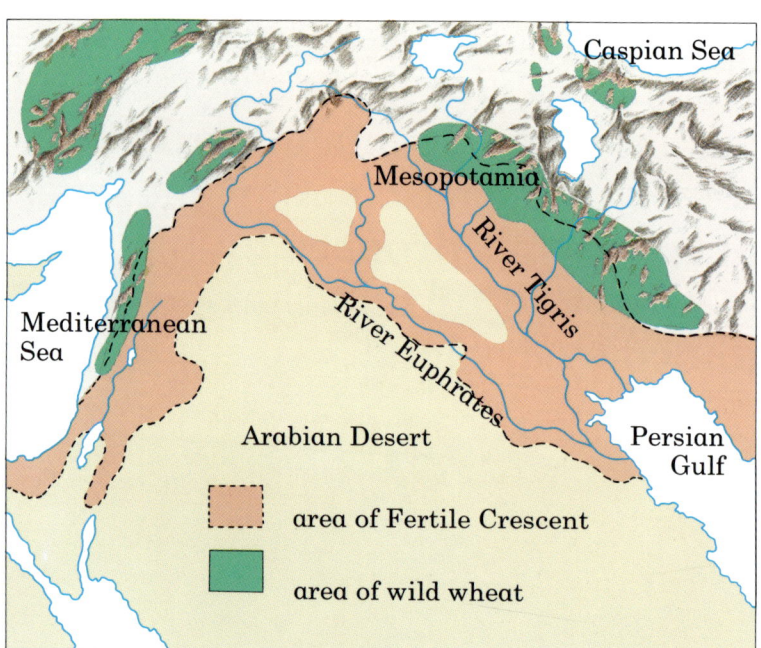

Caspian Sea
Mesopotamia
River Tigris
Mediterranean Sea
River Euphrates
Arabian Desert
Persian Gulf

area of Fertile Crescent

area of wild wheat

About 10,000 years ago, as the last Ice Age ended, wild wheat grew in the Middle East. In the warming climate, people planted this wheat in their homelands – an area known as the Fertile Crescent. They were the first people to be farmers.

The climate continued to warm over the next 5,000 years. Bamboo grew further north in China than ever before or since. In Europe, the warm weather brought clearer skies than today. People built stone circles which they could use to watch the Moon and stars.

About 4,000 years ago in Pakistan, cities were built in the Indus River valley where there was plenty of rain. But the climate became much drier and many people left the area. The cities became ruins.

▲ The Ring of Brodgar in Orkney was made about 4,500 years ago. It may have been used to watch the night sky which was probably clearer then.

▲ The ruins of a city in the Indus Valley. This is now a very dry area but 4,000 years ago, when people lived in the city, the climate was much wetter.

Climate from the Middle Ages

In the AD 300s, a warm period began in the areas between the Mediterranean Sea and the Equator. This made the farmland in the Middle East dry up. In North and Central America, the same warm weather may have helped the **Mayan Empire** grow.

Further north it was still cool. But in the 900s a warm spell made it possible for **Norse** people to settle in Greenland.

The frozen Thames

Some winters in England have been so cold that the River Thames froze. In London, people even had fairs on the ice! The biggest freeze happened in the winter of 1683-4, the middle of the Little Ice Age. The ice was 28 cm thick and a huge fair was held on it, with hundreds of stalls. People kept records of these winters and they help us study our past climate.

The Little Ice Age

From 1400 to 1800, there was a much cooler period, called the Little Ice Age. Greenland grew so cold again that the Norse settlements came to an end. In the 1600s, farmland in Sweden became too cold to grow crops and the people left. But the Little Ice Age also made the climate changeable. French wine harvest records, kept since the 1300s, show not only very cold years but also very hot ones.

Since the mid-1800s, most climates have been warmer. There have been some cold years, such as 1924 when the Baltic Sea froze, but most changes have been slight or for a short time.

◄ Some of the ways the world's climates have changed over the past 2,000 years:
1. The Mayan culture thrived in America when the climate was warmer from AD 250 to AD 900.
2. Norse settlers came to Greenland when its climate was warm enough to grow crops.
3. In the 1300s, severe storms caused flooding in large areas of northern Europe.
4. The largest of the fairs on the frozen River Thames in London. It was held in 1684 – during the Little Ice Age.
5. In 1846, warm wet weather in Ireland helped to spread a disease that rotted potatoes, causing famine.
6. In 1924, the Baltic Sea froze over. People could walk from Sweden to Denmark on the ice!

5

6

49

The Moving Deserts

▼ The yellow areas on this map show the desert regions of today. The brown areas show the regions in danger of becoming desert. People speed up this process by clearing away plants and failing to take proper care of the land.

The Sahara was not always the dry, sandy, rocky desert we know today. Rock paintings found there tell us that it was once green and wet. The paintings, made about 5,500 years ago, show cattle, antelope and crocodiles. One shows people hunting hippopotamus from a canoe! Where there is sand now, rivers once flowed and herds of animals fed on vast grasslands.

The Sahara dried up because the changes in climate after the Ice Age meant that little rain fell there. The rivers, plants and animals slowly disappeared.

Today, the Sahara is still growing. It is moving south into

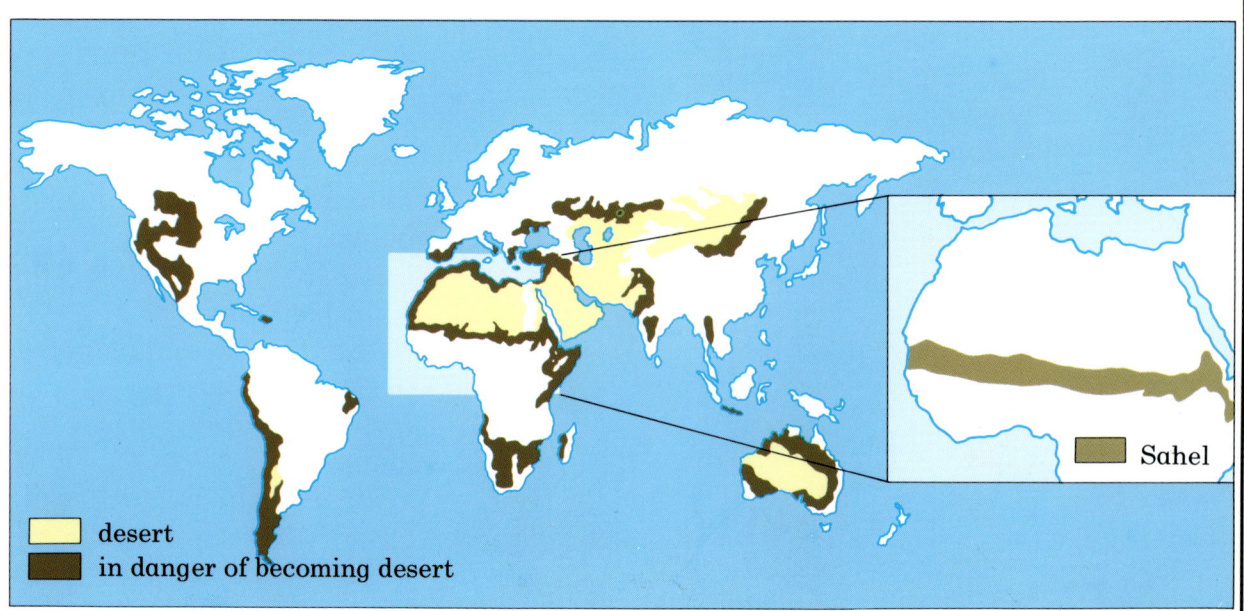

Sahel

desert
in danger of becoming desert

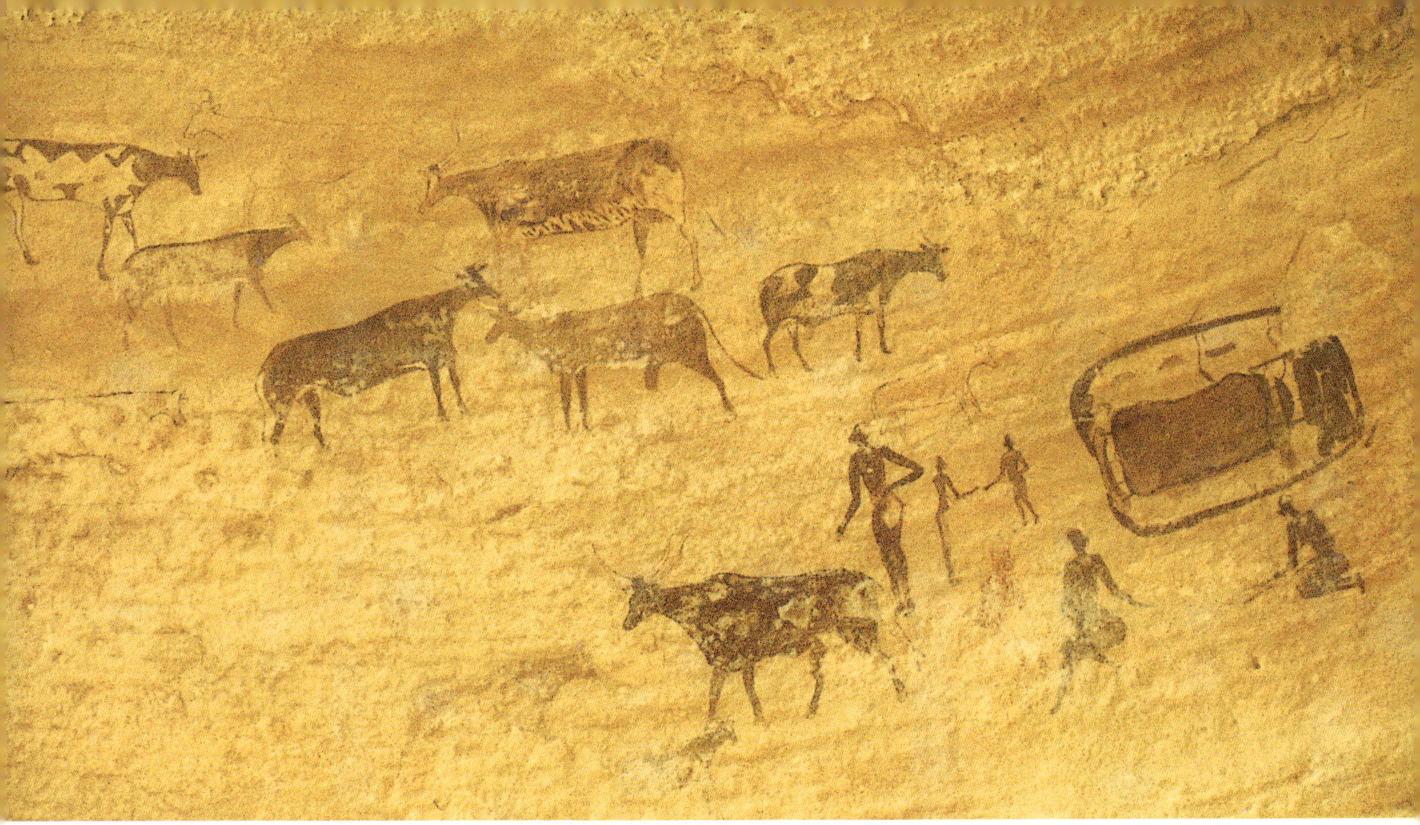

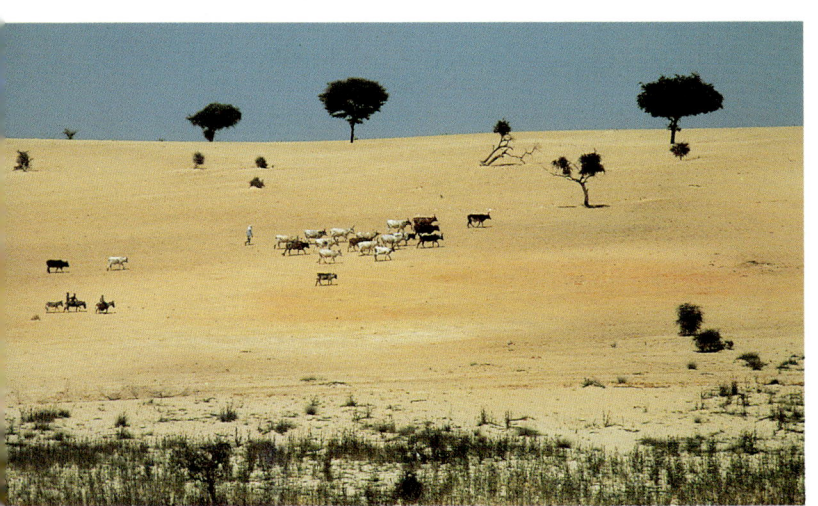

an area called the Sahel where not enough rain falls. In some parts of the Sahel, such as Ethiopia, crops can not grow and people are starving. As the map shows, other regions are also in danger of becoming desert from lack of rain – and people's actions.

▲ A rock painting from a mountain in the Sahara. It shows people tending cattle. It was painted long ago when the area was still grassland. Today, cattle could not live there.

Did you know?

The sand from the Sahara is sometimes blown as far as England, leaving a fine pale dust over cars and other surfaces.

◀ People herding cattle in the Sahel, just south of the Sahara. It is an area where rain does not often fall so the desert is spreading.

How People Change Climates

CHAPTER SIX

CLIMATE AND PEOPLE

Throughout the Earth's history, climates have changed from natural causes. But in the past 200 years, people have begun to change climates. In that time, the number of people has grown from fewer than 1,000 million to almost 5,500 million today.

With this huge increase in people, industry has also expanded widely. This has resulted in vast amounts of harmful chemicals, gases and smoke being pumped into the air we breathe. We call this dirtying of the air **pollution**.

Acid rain facts

- Acid rain is another result of people polluting the air.
- Acid rain falls from clouds in which chemicals produced by cars and factories have mixed with water vapour.
- Acid rain affects lakes and rivers so fish die. It also damages buildings, plants and the soil.

◄ Dust storms were one result of the Dust Bowl in the 1930s. They buried roads and houses.

The Dust Bowl

In the Great Plains of the United States, farmers ploughed up the native grasses that held the soil together. They planted wheat instead but this crop did not bind the soil so well. During the drought of the 1930s, winds blew away the soil. The area became known as the Dust Bowl.

◄ Opposite: dead trees surrounded by acid fog that helped kill them.

▼ Mexico City covered in smog. The city lies in a valley that traps car and factory pollution.

Smog

One type of pollution happens when fog and smoke mix together. This makes a very low, thick, dark cloud called smog. This is dangerous to most living things. In some large cities, such as Mexico City, Los Angeles and Athens, industry and cars have caused severe smogs.

People have also affected the climate by cutting down forests for firewood and to make space for crops. In drier areas, this can form deserts. Over half the world's forests have now been cut down.

The Greenhouse Effect

Top right: an iron and ◀ steel factory in China pouring out smoke full of carbon dioxide and other gases into the air.

What might happen?

If the greenhouse effect goes on, the Earth's climate will become much warmer. This may make the ice caps at the poles melt, raising the sea level and flooding places such as London and Tokyo.

Rainfall patterns may change. As a result, some green areas may become deserts.

We call the layer of air that surrounds the Earth the **atmosphere**. It is made up of different gases, including **carbon dioxide**. This gas helps trap the Sun's heat inside the atmosphere and keep the Earth warm. This is called the **greenhouse effect** because it is like the way a greenhouse traps heat for the plants growing inside it.

When fuels such as coal, oil and **natural gas** are burnt they give out carbon dioxide. In the past 200 years, people have burnt more and more of these fuels to run factories, cars and other machines. This has increased the amount of carbon dioxide in the air. As a result, the atmosphere's greenhouse effect is stronger and the Earth is warming up.

The Earth may be having one of its naturally warm periods. But many scientists think people are making the greenhouse effect stronger. If we do not reduce the amount of carbon dioxide our factories and cars make, the results could be disastrous.

Greenhouse gases

Carbon dioxide is not the only gas that causes the greenhouse effect. Other gases add to it. They are put into the atmosphere by people. Some of these gases are **chlorofluorocarbons**, or **CFCs**. Amongst other things, they are used in spray cans, refrigerators and foam packaging.

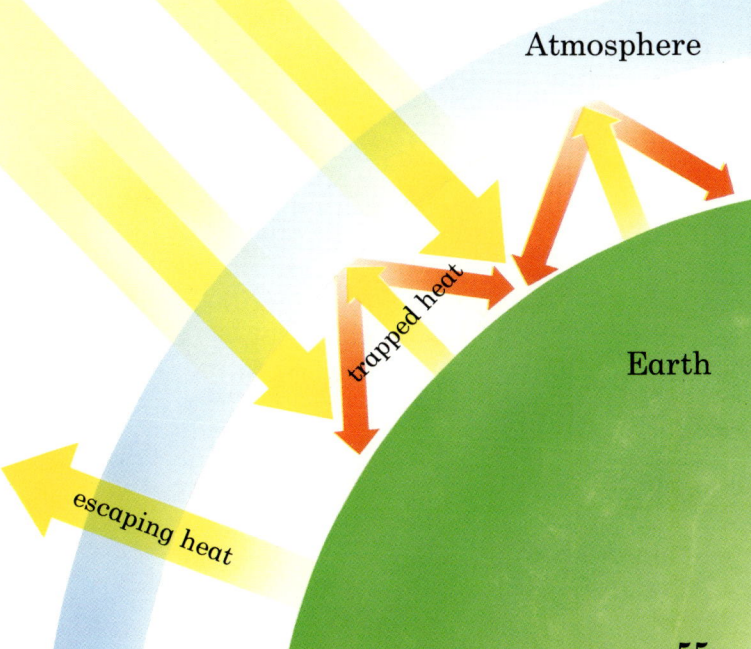

Sun's rays

Atmosphere

trapped heat

Earth

escaping heat

▶ How the greenhouse effect works: the Sun's rays warm the Earth's surface. Some of this warmth escapes into space but the rest of it is trapped by some of the gases in the atmosphere, such as carbon dioxide. The more of these gases there are, the less warmth escapes so the Earth gets warmer.

The Ozone Layer

Ozone is another gas found in the atmosphere. It forms in a layer around the Earth high above the ground. The ozone layer protects the Earth from **ultraviolet rays** given out by the Sun. These are invisible rays which are harmful to people as well as to plants and other animals.

In the early 1980s, scientists

► The two diagrams show the Antarctic ozone hole in the early 1980s and in 1989. The hole has grown a great deal in that time.

The dangers

If the ozone holes spread these could be some of the results:
● More people could develop skin cancer, cataracts and blindness.
● Some other diseases might spread faster.
● Acid smog might form.
● Food plants, such as rice, might not grow as well as they do today.

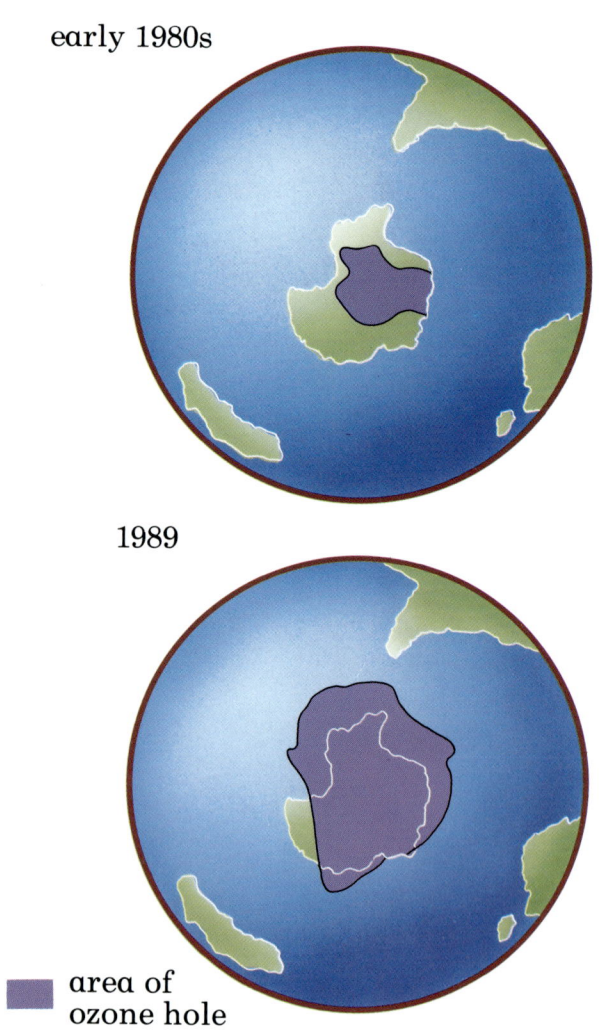

early 1980s

1989

area of ozone hole

discovered a hole in the ozone layer. It formed in Antarctica in spring (September to October there). Since then, the hole has appeared every spring and grown larger. Now, another hole has opened up over the Arctic.

Scientists think that these holes have been caused by CFCs – a short name for the gases called chlorofluorocarbons which also add to the greenhouse effect. CFCs break up ozone in the air.

In 1990, 50 countries agreed to stop making CFCs. But the effect of CFCs in the atmosphere will last up to 140 years. The danger to the ozone layer will be with us for a long time.

▲ The British Antarctic Survey Station in western Antarctica. Scientists working here were the first to find the ozone hole.

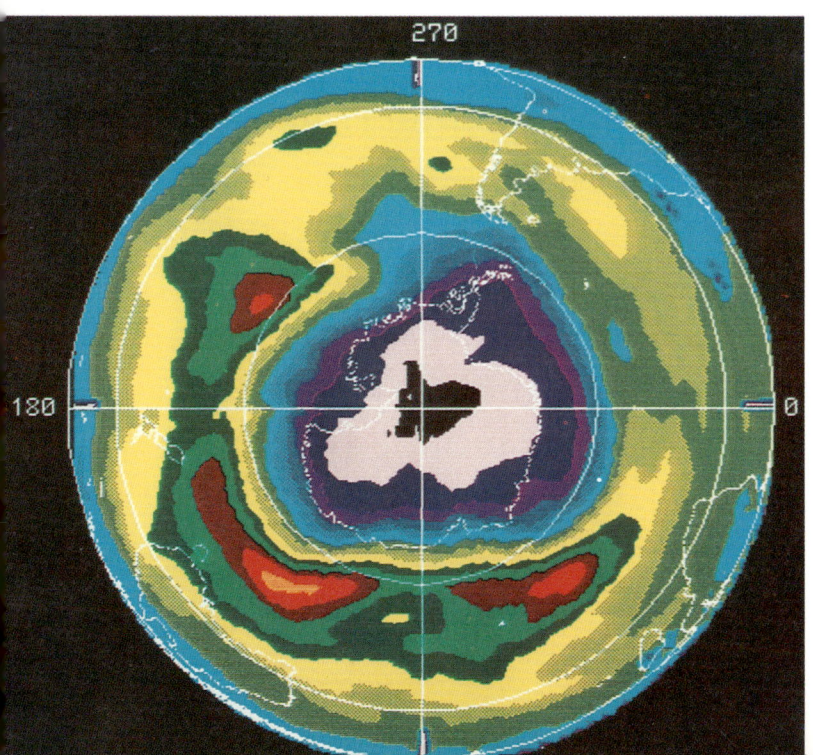

◄ This is a satellite picture which shows the spread of the Antarctic ozone hole. The pink and purple areas show where the ozone is thin. The black central area shows where it is thinnest.

Climate in the Future

► These fishing boats used to float on the Aral Sea. But the Aral has shrunk and the water is now several kilometres away. The boats have been left to rust and rot.

Sunny Britain?

If the world's climate does become warmer, the beaches in Britain might become as sunny as those in Spain. But some of the English beaches might disappear! The warming climate would melt some of the ice at the North Pole and the sea level would rise. This could flood parts of southern England for some kilometres inland.

The world's climate is changing. Africa's terrible droughts may be part of the change. But it is hard to tell by how much the climate is warming up.

We must study climate and its changes to see how they will affect our food supplies. We can then take steps to be sure that people of the future do not starve. At the same time, we must not upset the climate by our own actions. This means not only controlling air pollution but also planning ahead.

The Russians did not plan

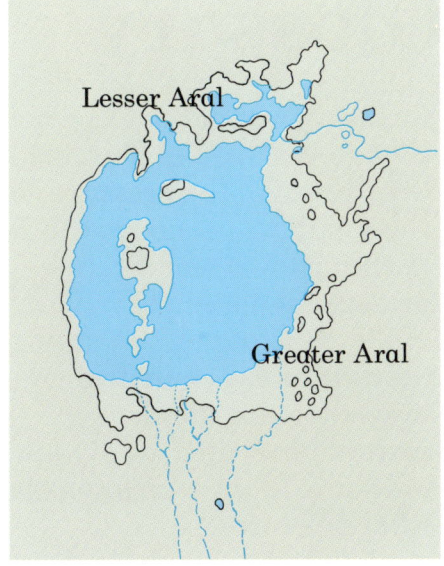

▲ The Aral sea today (the blue area) is in two parts. Its size in 1961 is outlined in black.

ahead when they used water from the rivers that flow into the Aral Sea to **irrigate** farmland. The Aral Sea began to shrink, its water became saltier and its fish died. Now, to correct the problem, there are plans to take water from rivers flowing into the Arctic Ocean. This might change the climate, perhaps bringing drought to Europe.

People's actions in one area can affect the climate in another. We must plan carefully if we want the Earth and its natural climate to survive.

▲ Starving people in Mali, Africa, being given food. The African famines have been caused by droughts which may be part of a change in climate.

Glossary

Air mass: one of the large bodies of air that moves around the world.

Air pressure: the pressure caused by the weight of air above the Earth pushing down on its surface. Air pressure is measured in bars or in millibars (1 bar = 1000 millibars).

Anemometer: an instrument used to measure wind speeds.

Anticyclone: an area of high air pressure. Light winds spiral outwards from its centre.

Atmosphere: the layer of air that surrounds the Earth.

Barometer: an instrument used to measure air pressure.

Cacti: the plural of cactus. A cactus is a desert plant with a thick, fleshy stem that stores water. It has spines instead of leaves.

Carbon dioxide: one of the gases in the air with no colour or smell. It is put into the air when animals breathe out and when any substance containing carbon burns. Plants use carbon dioxide to make their food.

Chlorofluorocarbons (CFCs): gases used by people in things such as spray cans and refrigerators. They damage the ozone layer.

Climatologist: a scientist who studies climates and how they change over a long time.

Condensation: what happens when a gas or vapour is changed into a liquid by cooling.

Cyclone: an area of low air pressure. Winds spiral in towards its centre.

Dinosaurs: a group of reptiles that lived on Earth long ago. The dinosaurs died out about 65 million years ago but we are not sure why this happened.

Evaporation: what happens when a liquid, such as water, is changed into a gas, by heat.

Front: the boundary on the ground between two air masses of different temperatures. Rain and clouds often gather along a front.

Glacial: a period of time, often called an ice age, when ice covered large areas of the Earth's surface.

Greenhouse effect: the way in which certain gases in the air, such as carbon dioxide, trap heat inside the Earth's atmosphere.

High: a short term for an area of high air pressure, or anticyclone. Light winds spiral outwards from its centre.

Humidity: the amount of water vapour in the air.

Interglacial: a period of time between two glacials or ice ages.

Irrigate: to water land and crops by using specially built channels and pipes. The water is taken from rivers or wells. Irrigation allows crops to be grown in dry places.

Isobars: these are lines which are drawn on weather maps. They link together points on the map which have the same air pressure.

Low: a short term to describe an area of low air pressure, or cyclone. Winds spiral slightly in towards its centre.

Mayan Empire: land in Central America ruled by the Maya people from about AD200 to AD900.

Meteorite: a mass of stone or metal that fell to Earth from space.

Meteorologist: a scientist who studies the day-to-day changes in the weather and what causes them.

Natural gas: a gas found naturally near underground oil. It is used as a fuel. When natural gas burns it gives out carbon dioxide.

Norse: this word describes the ancient peoples of Scandinavia (Sweden, Norway, Denmark and Iceland).

Occluded front: an occluded front forms when a warm air mass is caught between two cooler air masses and pushed above them.

Ozone: a pale blue gas with a sharp smell. It is found naturally in the Earth's upper atmosphere. Ozone filters out dangerous ultraviolent rays sent out by the Sun.

Poles: the two points (north and south) which mark the end of the line around which the Earth turns.

Pollution: the act of spoiling or poisoning any part of the land, sea or air. Pollution can result from things such as car exhaust fumes and chemical waste from factories.

Precipitation: this word describes all the different ways that water falls from the sky. The best known forms of precipitation are rain, hail and snow.

Prevailing wind: the wind that usually blows in a particular area.

Radar scanner: a machine that tracks the movement of objects, such as aeroplanes, and masses, such as rain clouds, in the sky.

Radiation balance: the overall amount of heat that a place on Earth gains or loses during a day.

Radiocarbon: a form of carbon found in very small amounts in all living things. After a living thing dies, its radiocarbon decays very slowly and at a constant rate.

Rain forest: a thick, evergreen forest found in the tropics. It has a good water supply all year round.

Satellite: a body that goes around a larger body in space. The Earth is a satellite of the Sun. There are satellites made by people that circle around the Earth. Communication satellites are used to send radio and TV signals around the world. Weather satellites give information about the weather on Earth which they watch from space.

Static electricity: electricity that builds up on the surface of materials that do not allow electricity to flow through them.

Sunspot: a dark patch seen on the surface of the Sun. Sunspots last only a few weeks or months, and tend to appear in bursts of activity every eleven years.

Temperate: neither very hot nor very cold. Most of Europe has a temperate climate.

Temperature: the amount of hotness or coldness of something. Temperature is usually measured in degrees Celsius with a thermometer.

Thermometer: an instrument that measures temperature.

Tropics: the area of land on either side of the Equator and between the Tropic of Cancer and the Tropic of Capricorn. The climate of the tropics is always warm or hot.

Ultraviolet rays: invisble rays which occur in sunlight. Ultraviolet rays can cause sunburn in hot clear weather.

Vapour: a gas that forms from a liquid or a solid. Water vapour in the air may turn into the water droplets that make up clouds.

Weather system: a pattern of highs and lows which are linked together, and the weather that results from this pattern.

Index

A number in **bold** shows the entry is illustrated on that page. The same page often has writing about the entry too.